AMERICAN VOICES

JAPANESE AMERICANS

AMERICAN VOICES

JAPANESE AMERICANS

by **Fred S. Rolater**
and **Jeannette Baker Rolater**

Rourke Corporation, Inc.
Vero Beach, Florida 32964

Cover photo: Kimberly Dawson

∞The paper used in this book conforms to the American National Standard for Permanence of Paper for
Printed Library Materials, Z39.48-1984.

Library of Congress Cataloging-in-Publication Data
Rolater, Fred S., 1938-
   Japanese Americans/Fred S. Rolater, Jeannette
Baker Rolater.
       p.   cm.—(American voices)
   Includes bibliographical references and index.
   Summary: Discusses Japanese who have
immigrated to the United States, their reasons for
coming, where they have settled, and how they have
contributed to their new country.
   ISBN 0-86593-138-0
   1. Japanese Americans—Juvenile literature. 2.
Japanese Americans—Biography—Juvenile literature.
[1. Japanese Americans.] I. Rolater, Jeannette Baker,
1938-   . II. Title. III. Series.
E184.J3R65 1991   91-15807
973'.04956—dc20   CIP
                                            AC

CONTENTS

THE JAPANESE IN

NORTH AMERICA

More than 800,000 people of Japanese descent live in the United States, according to the 1990 census. Although Asian Americans as a whole constitute the fastest growing ethnic group in the United States, Japanese Americans comprise a declining proportion of the Asian-American community. In 1970, Japanese Americans were the largest Asian-American group; in 1980, they ranked third behind the Chinese and Filipino populations; and preliminary 1990 census figures show that they are probably ranked no higher than fourth or fifth. Japanese emigrants have not contributed substantially to the new surge in Asian immigration, primarily because Japan's economic prosperity in recent decades has encouraged many of its citizens to remain at home. Japanese Americans who live in the United States and Canada today are, for the most part, descendants of immigrants who first arrived on American shores just before the turn of the century. The record of their past century in North America is a story of a proud people with ancient cultural traditions learning to adapt and succeed in a new world that was eager for their labor but often hostile to their efforts to settle and become citizens.

COMING TO AMERICA

The first Japanese came to Hawaii in 1868, to California in 1869, and to Canada in 1886. Today they are often regarded as

U.S. Public Health Service officers make a quarantine inspection of passengers on a trans-Pacific passenger liner from Japan, February, 1924.

a model minority for their high valuation of education, their strong work habits, low crime rate and high income. The original Issei, or first-generation Japanese immigrants, worked in the Hawaiian sugarcane and pineapple fields and on the railroads, in the canneries, and in the logging areas on the West Coast of the United States and Canada.

These immigrants were often the targets of racial discrimination. In 1907 the *San Francisco Chronicle* announced, "The Japanese are not liked, nor desired here. We do not see why they do not all clear out and go to Los Angeles or Boston, Mass." Their physical characteristics made them a visibly distinct population in areas of the United States and Canada where anti-Asian sentiment had first been directed at Chinese immigrants. Labor unions, local politicians, and newspapers exploited this racial prejudice for their own ends and claimed the influx of Japanese immigrants represented a new episode of "yellow peril" which would cause Caucasians to lose their employment, their housing, and even their culture. Beginning in 1913, California passed a law prohibiting Japanese residents—"aliens ineligible for citizenship"—from owning land. Between 1942 and 1945, Japanese Americans on the mainland—including second-generation United States citizens of Japanese descent—were placed in internment camps in the West and in Arkansas, closed in with barbed wire, and treated as prisoners. Yet at the same time, most Japanese Americans in Hawaii were not interned. The 442nd Combat Team, made up entirely of Nisei volunteers, served in Italy and France and became the most decorated regimental-sized unit in any American war.

Postwar American society became more tolerant in its attitudes toward ethnic minorities. In the late 1940's and early 1950's, new legislation and favorable court decisions overturned many of the legal restrictions that had prevented Issei and other Asian-born residents from becoming naturalized citizens, from owning land, and from marrying non-Asians. The Civil Rights movement of the 1960's helped eliminate other racial barriers that prevented Japanese citizens from sharing equally in American society. Many Japanese Americans worked hard to gain recognition and compensation for the indignities they had suffered during World War II. These changes improved the life of many Japanese Americans. Perhaps astronaut Ellison Onizuka, killed in the *Challenger* explosion in 1986, best described the struggle of Japanese immigrants to America in comments he made after his flight on the space shuttle *Discovery* in 1985:

> I looked down as we passed over Hawaii and thought about all the sacrifices of all the people who helped me along the way. My grandparents, who were contract laborers; my parents, who did without to send me to college; my school teachers, coaches, and ministers—all the past generations who pulled together to create the present. Different people, different races, different religions—all working toward a common goal, all one family.

CULTURAL BONDS: THE JAPANESE LANGUAGE

The Japanese language was the original common bond of all Japanese Americans. The original Japanese immigrants had a difficult time learning to speak English and many Issei spoke only Japanese at home. Over the years, many Japanese Americans have lost this bilingual ability, with the result that Japanese-American children often go to school to learn Japanese. It is one of the most beautiful spoken languages in the world. Like Italian, all Japanese syllables end in one of the five vowels except for a few that have an "n" on the end such as *yon*, a term meaning "four." Their vowels are a (ah), e (pronounced like a long a), i (ee), o (oh), and u (oo). Most of the consonants sound the same as they do in English but l and r are difficult for the Japanese since these letters are not used much and sound almost like a soft d. Learning to speak Japanese is relatively easy since it is so musical but the speaker must remember to give every syllable an equal stress. Thus, the name Loleita (the Japanese version of Rolater) is not pronounced LO′lei•ta but lo•lei•ta. Japanese pronunciation makes many terms sound different than they would in English. The automobile corporation named Mitsubishi should be pronounced Mi•tsu•bi•shi, not Mit•su•bi•shi. The motorcycle and automobile corporation named Honda is pronounced Hohn•da, not Hahn•da as we say it in English. The name Yamashita is actually pronounced Ya•mash•ta. Although pronunciation of Japanese words can be challenging, learning to read Japanese is even more difficult since the Japanese use three ways of writing. One form is called *kangi*, in which Chinese characters represent entire words. The other two forms of writing are syllabaries in which the symbols represent individual syllables. These forms are *hiragana* (used for Japanese words) and *katakana* (used for foreign words).

FESTIVE CELEBRATIONS

Besides the Japanese language, another legacy of Japanese culture in North America is found in the many festivals held at various times during the year. Four are most popular among Japanese Americans. The first is O-shogatsu, or New Year's. It lasts three days from January 1 through 3. Everyone has a great time since happiness during this celebration is thought to continue through the whole year. Mochi, a special rice cake, and noodles are served for supper. Fireworks displays are often part of the festivities.

The next two festivals revolve around children. The first is Hinamatsuri, or Girl's Day, on March 3. Each girl has a special set of dolls which she dresses and displays for her friends who come to visit. Many have twenty-five or more dolls including very fancy ones representing the emperor and

Girls Day is enjoyed by three friends, dressed in traditional clothing, as they play in front of an elaborate doll display.

empress of Japan. On May 5, families celebrate Tango-no-sekku, or Boy's Day. Families fly kites in the shape of a carp (a type of fish), usually one for each boy in the family. The carp stands for courage and endurance.

In August, many Japanese Americans celebrate O-Bon, often called the Festival of the Lanterns in America. It is the special week in Japan for Buddhists to honor their ancestors. In the United States and Canada, the families go to churches, temples, or shrines and place flowers on the graves of their ancestors. Most families also show their reverence for their ancestors by visiting their oldest living relatives. For this reason, O-Bon is often considered to be the favorite festival of the grandparents.

RELIGIOUS TRADITIONS

Religious culture is another rich component of Japanese-American life. The oldest of the Japanese religions is Shinto. It is an agricultural and warrior religion that emphasizes strong family ties. Almost every Shinto family has their own family shrine honoring the *kami* or spirits of their ancestors. Shinto believers also worship at public shrines, many of which are noted for their beauty and have become popular tourist attractions in Japan. Although there is no organized church, Shinto practices endure in modern times. Traditional Japanese weddings in Japan and in America are conducted according to Shinto rites.

In A.D. 522 Buddhism arrived in Japan from India by way of China and Korea. Buddhist teachings show believers how to deal with a constantly changing world by emphasizing a way of inner peace for each individual. In Japan as well as in China, Confucian philosophy was also attached to Buddhism. Confucian teachings emphasize harmony in society and endurance as the key to success. Temples and monasteries provide places of worship and contemplation for Buddhists, and many Buddhist temples can be found in Hawaii and in Japanese-American communities on the mainland. Most Japanese are buried in Buddhist ceremonies and many families adhere to Buddhist as well as Shinto precepts, even in America.

Christianity came to Japan with Portuguese traders and Catholic missionaries in 1545 and had much early influence among the Japanese. Because it became entangled with politics and foreign intrigue, Christianity in its Catholic and Protestant

In a mix of old and new, Eastern and Western, the traditional wedding kimono is still favored by most brides, while grooms usually prefer formal Western attire.

forms was forbidden in Japan for some 250 years until the late nineteenth century. Today, many prominent Japanese are Christians, but they comprise only 2 percent of the overall population of Japan. In contrast, perhaps one-third to one-half of all Japanese Americans have become Christians. Although some have joined mainstream congregations, others still worship in their own Japanese congregations. Some Japanese Americans have returned to Japan as missionaries for various Christian denominations.

FOOD FROM THE HOMELAND

Another common thread among Japanese-American families is Japanese food. Though hamburgers, peanut butter, and fried chicken are very popular, so are the traditional Japanese foods of o-sushi, sashimi, tempura, yakitori, and sukiyaki. Most Americans think that sushi means raw fish, but it actually refers to anything served "with rice." Many different types of sushi can be served with the special vinegar rice. One of the favorites is sashimi, which consists of thin slices of raw squid, octopus, flounder, tuna, shrimp, or other seafood served with the sushi rice and wasabi, a type of very hot ground-up radish. Yaki means meat, and yakitori is one type of quick-fried meat dish. Sukiyaki refers to strips of beef, vegetables, noodles, and tofu (soybean curd) cooked quickly in a special sauce made from soybeans and sugar. Tempura is an American favorite. It consists of deep-fried seafood and vegetables which have been dipped in a special batter. The two traditional Japanese beverages are o-cha, or green tea, and sake (pronounced sah•kee). Green tea is always drunk hot and the better varieties are naturally sweet requiring no sugar. Sake is a type of rice wine usually served hot in small porcelain cups. Desserts usually consist of fruit. For Japanese Americans, the favorites include strawberries, pineapple, oranges, apples, and mikon, which is a type of tangerine.

FOUR GENERATIONS IN AMERICA

Like other immigrant groups, there are changes from one generation to another among Japanese Americans. For the Japanese Americans the changes have been so prominent that the generations have special names. Three names correspond to the Japanese names for the counting numbers one through three: *ichi*, *ni*, *san*. Instead of using *shi*, the Japanese counting number for four, the term *yon*, also meaning four, is used. The generations are the Issei, Nisei, Sansei, and Yonsei. The Issei were the original immigrants who first arrived in Hawaii, the mainland United States, and Canada between 1868 and 1924. The Nisei were their children, the first Japanese-American citizens, born in America between 1900 and 1940. Their children, the third-generation Sansei, were born in the postwar baby boom period from 1945 to 1965, and the Yonsei or newest fourth generation are just now entering college and the work force.

THE COMMUNITY

The Japanese-American community has been largely defined by the activities of the four generations described in the previous chapter. The Issei were born in Japan and came to the United States between 1868 and 1924; their education and family background emphasized conformity, group loyalty, family obligations, and quiet acceptance of one's status in life. The Nisei were born in the United States between 1900 and 1940 and were citizens by birth. Their knowledge of English was much superior to their Japanese, and many had the opportunity to attend college and receive advanced degrees. These first two generations endured much discrimination. The Sansei, born during the period from the 1940's to the 1960's, have been more easily assimilated into American society and have had greater opportunities for success than their parents. Their children, the Yonsei, are by far the most Americanized of the four generations. From Issei to Yonsei, the Japanese-American community has undergone enormous changes while maintaining its distinctive culture.

JAPANTOWNS AND LITTLE TOKYOS

The early Japanese contract laborers in Hawaii and the United States were housed and fed on the plantations and farms where they worked. Because conditions were often poorer than what they were accustomed to in their homeland, these Japanese workers banded together to assist each other and lobby for better treatment. Japanese immigrants who arrived later were generally not under obligation to a single employer. These workers were expected to find their own

Japantowns and Little Tokyos in America integrate Japanese and Western tastes, as exemplified by this pizza shop in Little Tokyo, Los Angeles, California, 1991.

housing. Denied housing in certain areas because of their race and their economic situation, many of these workers formed their own Japanese communities within larger cities near where they worked. These communities—called Little Tokyos and Japantowns (*Nihonmachis*)—offered Issei workers cheap lodgings and other amenities in an environment where language and cultural barriers did not exist.

These ethnic communities allowed Issei workers and businessmen to maintain their Japanese culture by establishing their own schools, churches, stores, restaurants, and social networks. Men who shared the same jobs helped each other to save funds to bring wives, families, and other relatives over from Japan. Many social networks grew out of the close friendships which had developed between Japanese workers and their families who traveled on the same ship to communities in the United States and Canada.

The Nisei, or second-generation Japanese Americans, had a better command of English and had the benefits of an American education. Many of them hoped that their education would provide them with greater economic opportunities outside their Japanese communities. Faced with the same racial discrimination that their parents had experienced (although often in subtler forms), many Nisei decided to devote themselves to their family's businesses and used their educational skills to expand Japanese-American farms, gardening businesses, stores, and other business enterprises.

WORLD WAR II AND INTERNMENT

December 7, 1941, became a day of great change within the Japanese-American community. At dawn the Japanese naval forces struck Pearl Harbor, Hawaii, and the United States entered World War II. On December 8, the FBI began arresting 2,191 prominent Issei who were suspected of loyalty to the Japanese government. Though these arrests created a leadership problem, the Japanese-American community reluctantly accepted the action and hoped that those arrested would be released quickly. At first, this seemed to be the only action that would be taken, since the War Department did not seriously believe that the Japanese would invade the West Coast. The Japanese Americans in Hawaii allayed fears about their loyalty by providing assistance in the cleanup after the Japanese attack. In fact there were already 1,543 Americans of Japanese ancestry, one-third of them volunteers, in the armed forces in Hawaii, and Japanese Americans there were extremely supportive of the American war effort.

However, by January, 1942, invasion fears increased and a storm of demands began for the removal of all Japanese Americans from the West Coast states of California, Washington, and Oregon. The principal supporters of removal included the newspapers, certain politicians, labor unions, and various nativist groups. Fears of Japanese invasion were not the only reason these groups supported removal. Many of them had a general distrust of all immigrants, feared economic competition by Japanese-American workers and by "cheap" Japanese manufactured goods, and were easily persuaded to suspect the loyalties of an identifiable racial group. President Franklin Roosevelt gave in to the pressure and on February 19, 1942, issued Executive Order 9066 without consulting either Congress or his cabinet. It authorized the "evacuation" of all persons of Japanese descent from California, Oregon, and Washington. The original order called for close supervision of German and Italian Americans in these same states, yet neither of these more numerous groups were interned, primarily because they could not be easily identified on sight. In Hawaii, where nearly 40 percent of the population was Japanese, there was no evacuation. On March 2, the army ordered the evacuation of all Japanese persons from the western half of California, Oregon, and Washington, as well as the southern

Manzanar Relocation Camp, located east of Fresno, California, was just one of many Japanese internment camps in the Western United States and Canada used during World War II.

third of Arizona. This order affected 110,000 of the 126,000 Japanese in the continental United States. Of those affected, 70,000 were American citizens deprived of their rights without legal action or evidence of disloyalty.

All evacuees were assembled at designated reporting centers, the best known of which was Santa Anita Race Track in Los Angeles. Families were allowed to take with them only what they could carry, including clothing, bedding and linens, toilet articles, and eating utensils such as forks, spoons, knives, and bowls. Some entrusted their additional belongings and property to non-Japanese friends, but most were forced to sell all that they owned for very low prices. Their bank accounts were frozen and many had to abandon their farms or lease them to non-Japanese workers.

By August 7, 1942, these Japanese evacuees had been assembled at the reporting centers and were moved by train and bus to ten internment camps. The following chart shows the locations and sizes of these internment camps, eight of which were built on government-owned desert land in the West with two others in Arkansas.

WORLD WAR II JAPANESE INTERNMENT CAMPS IN THE UNITED STATES

Camp Name	Location	Capacity
Manzanar	Central California	10,000
Tule Lake	Northern California	16,000
Poston	Western Arizona	20,000
Gila	Southern Arizona	15,000
Topaz	Utah	10,000
Minidoka	Idaho	10,000
Heart Mountain	Wyoming	12,000
Granada	Colorado	8,000
Jerome	Southeastern Arkansas	10,000
Rohwer	Southeastern Arkansas	10,000

Source: Robert A. Wilson and Bill Hosokawa, *East to America: A History of the Japanese in the United States* (New York: William Morrow, 1980), p. 212.

In a typical camp for ten thousand people, there were thirty-six blocks. In each block were twelve barracks, each designed to hold about twenty-four individuals in six families. Each family unit was a bare room twenty feet square with only army cots and blankets. There was no other furniture, no running water, and no kitchen facilities. Each block had a mess hall, which prepared food for the residents, and a

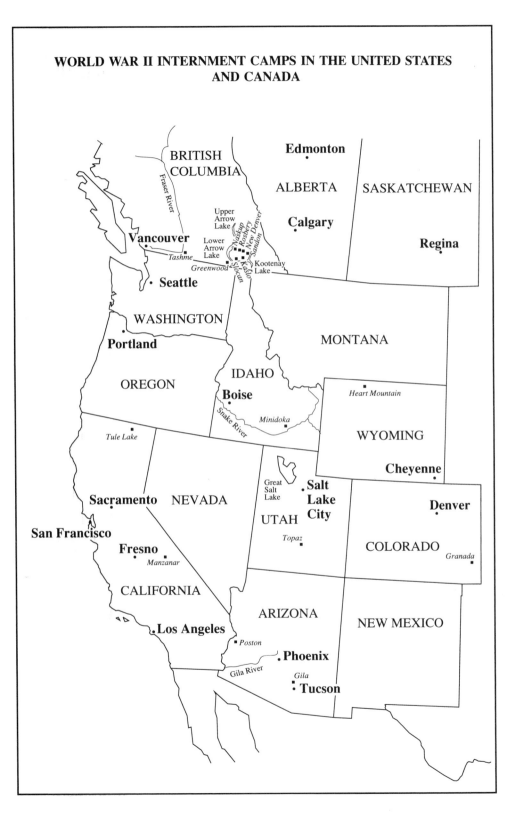

WORLD WAR II INTERNMENT CAMPS IN THE UNITED STATES AND CANADA

recreation hall, usually an empty barracks with no furniture. At first the camps were surrounded by barbed wire fences and armed guards, but later the fences were removed as the Japanese Americans proved to be extremely cooperative. The residents struggled to preserve some semblance of normalcy in the camps. Elementary and high schools were opened for the children and young adults. Social events such as dances became common, and many older adults turned to artistic endeavors such as learning the Japanese tea ceremony, kabuki dance, or flower arranging.

The government later allowed the Japanese in the camps to take an oath of allegiance to the United States, ending all allegiance to Japan or any foreign power. This oath created great tension within families. The Issei—who were unable to become American citizens—were reluctant to renounce their Japanese citizenship, but many took the oath anyway. The Nisei, on the other hand, were eager to reaffirm their citizenship. Some 35,000 of the Nisei, mostly younger males and females, moved to work in war industries and other necessary jobs in the East and the Midwest beginning in January, 1943. After the war, some of them moved back to the West Coast to live, but the majority stayed to become the first large group of Japanese Americans in those areas. In 1945 most of the Japanese Americans who had remained in the internment camps moved back to their former homes on the West Coast.

On June 25, 1943, Marion Konishi, Citizen Number 6E-12-D, spoke as class valedictorian at the graduation of the high school at Granada camp. Her speech articulates the great anguish experienced by the Japanese-American community as a whole and for Nisei citizens in particular during the war:

> One and a half years ago I knew only one America—an America that gave me an equal chance in the struggle for life, liberty, and the pursuit of happiness. If I were asked

then—"What does America mean to you?"—I would
answer without any hesitation and with all sincerity—
"America means freedom, equality, security, and justice."
The other night while I was preparing for this speech, I
asked myself this same question—"What does America
mean to you?" I hesitated—I was not sure of my answer. I
wondered if America still means and will mean freedom,
equality, security, and justice when some of its citizens were
segregated, discriminated against, and treated so unfairly. I
knew I was not the only American seeking an answer.

JAPANESE-AMERICAN TROOPS IN WORLD WAR II

More than 1,500 Japanese Americans were serving in the
United States Army in Hawaii on December 7, 1941. In June,
1942 with the Japanese threat to the islands diminished, these
troops were sent to the mainland to train as the 100th Infantry
Battalion. They were in final training at Camp Shelby,
Mississippi, when on February 1, 1943, President Roosevelt
ordered the establishment of the 442nd Regimental Combat
Team, an all-Nisei unit whose second and third battalions were
recruited both in Hawaii and in the internment camps on the
mainland.

The unit fought in Italy from September, 1943, to
September, 1944; was then sent to fight in Southern France;
and finally returned to complete their duty in Italy. The 442nd
became the most decorated regimental unit in American
history in any war: The 18,000 individual decorations awarded
to the unit included one Congressional Medal of Honor, won
by Sadao S. Munemori, fifty-two Distinguished Service
Crosses, one Distinguished Service Medal, nearly 600 Silver
Stars, more than 5,000 Bronze Stars, and 9,500 Purple Hearts.
As a unit, the 442nd won forty-three Division commendations,
thirteen Army commendations, and seven Presidential
Distinguished Unit Citations. It was truly said that some of the
veterans could not even wear all their decorations on their
uniforms.

19

An all-Nisei unit in World War II was the most decorated regimental unit in American history.

The service of Japanese Americans in the Pacific theater during World War II is less known but equally important. More than 6,000 Nisei, including many Kibei (Nisei who were educated in Japan and returned to America) graduated from the Military-Intelligence Language School. They were assigned as interpreters to American and Australian units throughout the Pacific. Their translations, often obtained under fire and close to the Japanese lines, saved many American lives and shortened the war. The performance of Japanese-American soldiers was instrumental in earning respect for their entire community in postwar American society.

JAPANESE IN WARTIME CANADA

The situation was as bad if not worse in Canada. That country had entered World War II in Europe in August, 1939, with the rest of the British Commonwealth. In December, 1941, all Japanese in Canada were required to register as enemy aliens even though 75 percent were Canadian citizens by birth or naturalization. In January all males between the ages of 18 to 45 were sent to detention camps at least 100 miles inland, and the next month all Japanese in the country were moved. Housing was very poor and schooling not available for the children at first. Eventually many camp residents were allowed to move to eastern Canada to work.

Resumption of normal life for the Japanese Canadians came slowly but inexorably also. There was continued opposition to their presence in British Columbia. Some 4,000 left voluntarily for Japan, where they found little welcome but some jobs with the occupation forces as translators. Others were encouraged to migrate to eastern Canada. Finally protests by civil rights groups, some white politicians, and the Japanese forced the closing of the camps in 1947. A compensation bill was passed; it paid about 23 percent of the total losses incurred by Japanese Canadians, more than double the American average.

Japanese Canadians were given the right to vote in 1948 in federal elections, and British Columbia allowed them to vote in local elections in 1949. Japanese immigrants were again permitted to come to Canada in 1950 and Japanese rights to Canadian citizenship were restored.

POSTWAR CIVIL RIGHTS EFFORTS

Legal opposition to the evacuations began early. On December 18, 1944, the U.S. Supreme Court in the *Endo* case ruled that there was no legal basis for the indefinite detention of loyal Americans of Japanese descent. One day before the ruling the military authorities had authorized all detainees to begin returning to their homes. Despite the fear that had caused the evacuations, no Japanese American was ever charged with disloyal acts towards the American government.

Problems with discrimination still remained in California. In 1946 the California Supreme Court unanimously upheld the right of the state to seize the property of Kajiro Oyama, an Issei who had bought land in the name of his citizen son, Fred. But the tide began to turn when the U.S. Supreme Court reversed that decision two years later. Proposition 15 on the California ballot in 1946 would have made the Alien Land Law part of the state constitution. It was overwhelmingly defeated by the voters. Then in 1948, the California Supreme Court ruled that interracial marriages were legal in the state; in 1967, the U.S. Supreme Court said the same thing for all the nation.

Led by Mike Masaoka, their first lobbyist in Washington, the Japanese American Citizens League (JACL) began a determined drive to provide for equality and justice for Japanese Americans. Their first victory was the Soldier's Bride Act of 1947, which allowed American soldiers to marry in Japan and bring their wives to the United States. Masaoka soon found powerful allies in Washington, including

Congressmen Walter Judd of Minnesota and Francis Walter of Pennsylvania and Senator Pat McCarran of Nevada. Then in 1948 President Harry Truman's Civil Rights program included several important measures for the Japanese. Citizenship was extended to all aliens who had served in the American armed forces in World War I or World War II, "irrespective of race." Another bill allowed many Japanese businessmen, students, wives, and others who had stayed in the United States during the war to seek permanent residency rather than go back to Japan. Finally Congress passed a law allowing compensation to the evacuees during the War Relocation.

Unfortunately the Department of Justice, which administered the claims program for the evacuees, was very stringent, and only about 10 percent of the real losses were ever paid. But the symbolism of apology and payment was of great psychological importance to the evacuees, who felt their rights as citizens had been restored. (Subsequent protests by the younger members of the Japanese-American community led the JACL to appoint a committee in 1978 to seek redress for the insult of relocation in the form of an apology and a payment in money. Finally, after ten years, in August, 1988, the "Apology" bill became law, granting $20,000 to each of the survivors of the internment camps.)

In 1952, the JACL and its friends in Congress passed the McCarran-Walter Act, which in effect repealed the Oriental Exclusion Act of 1924 and the Gentlemen's Agreement before that. The McCarran-Walter Act allowed a token immigration quota to all Asian nations, 185 a year to Japan, and removed all racial barriers to naturalization as citizens. By 1965, 46,000 Issei had become United States citizens.

In 1965, President Lyndon Johnson signed into law a new immigration act which eliminated all references to national origins. Priority for immigration was to be based on relationship to American citizens and to persons who held needed job skills. The Japanese were now eligible for free migration to the United States for the first time since 1907.

THE HAWAIIAN COMMUNITY

By World War II, Japanese Americans made up 40 percent of the Hawaiian population. Even with large-scale migration from the mainland United States in recent years, Japanese Americans make up 25 percent of the population, by far the largest single ethnic group. Names such as Kitano, Inouye, Matsunaga, and Ariyoshi are as common in Hawaii as Smith or Jones on the mainland. Like the Irish in Boston or the Germans in Milwaukee, the Japanese in Hawaii play a leading role in business and politics.

Distinctive Japanese cultural traditions are maintained in Hawaii as well. The Cherry Blossom Festival in the spring celebrates Japanese contributions in much the way of Japan but includes a parade with a Japanese-American queen. Japanese language schools are still active, but attendance is declining among Sansei and Yonsei, who see little reason for learning the language of their parents and grandparents. In contrast, the Japanese-American courses at the University of Hawaii developed by Professor Dennis Ogawa are widely attended. There are numbers of beautiful Shinto shrines and Buddhist temples. New Year's and O-Bon are commonly celebrated.

JAPANESE CULTURE IN CALIFORNIA

The Japanese-American population in California is concentrated in the Los Angeles basin, the San Francisco Bay Area, and in Sacramento. Although Little Tokyos still exist in Los Angeles and San Francisco, few American-born citizens live in these communities, and the number of new arrivals from Japan is not large enough to replenish their population.

Important Japanese-American cultural events in California

David Fowler

Representing the pride, strength, honor, and accomplishments of the Japanese-American community, this memorial to Ellison S. Onizuka, astronaut on the space shuttle Challenger, *stands in Little Tokyo, Los Angeles, California.*

include the Nisei Parade in Los Angeles and various events at the ethnic churches. There are thirty-four active Japanese churches of the Southern California Ministerial Fellowship (a Japanese body), and Buddhist and Christian ministers meet regularly on items of mutual interest. Business and social organizations such as the Los Angeles Optimists, the Los Angeles and San Francisco Japanese Junior Chambers of Commerce, and the Nikkei Lions have been established to promote awareness of Japanese-American interests and concerns. (Nikkei is a word designating all Japanese Americans as opposed to Issei, Nisei, Sansei, and Yonsei, which refer to specific generations.)

Although the Little Tokyos are in decline, some suburban communities in California retain a Japanese flavor. The communities of Gardena and Torrance, southwest of Los Angeles, have large concentrations of Japanese Americans who appear to be fully assimilated but maintain their social ties with other Japanese Americans. From their veterans and senior citizens centers to their Sansei baseball league and Miss Nisei Week beauty pageant, these communities have special organizations that allow Japanese-American residents to socialize with each other and maintain their ethnic heritage.

EAST OF THE MISSISSIPPI

Japanese-Americans living east of the Mississippi have not concentrated in specific ethnic neighborhoods, although most do live in urban communities. Often the center of the community grows from the activities of a particular social organization. Some of these organizations resemble those found in Gardena, California. One organization is designed to accommodate the children of the Japanese corporate representatives. Often used before World War II to teach the Japanese language and culture to the Nisei, Japanese supplementary schools have become active again. Now, partially funded by the Japanese Ministry of Education, they are found in many eastern states. One such organization meets at Middle Tennessee State University, in Murfreesboro, Tennessee. It teaches Japanese language, culture, history, and mathematics on Saturdays to the sons and daughters of "temporary" immigrants in order to prepare them to reenter school in Japan. Math is especially necessary since the Japanese system is always one to two years in advance of the American system in that subject.

JAPAN

To understand the Japanese Americans, it is important to understand their cultural origins and to learn essential facts about their homeland. The rich history of Japan has particular significance in explaining Japanese immigrants' decisions to leave. This same history also has affected their lives in America: their destinations in the United States and Canada, their reception upon their arrival, and their attitudes, careers, and success here.

THE LANDSCAPE OF JAPAN

Japan is one of the most beautiful countries in the world, a land of sea and mountains, of shimmering blue and emerald green much of the year. It is a land of contrasts: of wild mountains with little or no population as well as cities that are among the most densely populated areas in the world; a land of great wealth and intense poverty.

Nippon or Nihon, as the Japanese call it, is located in the North Pacific Ocean off the northeast coast of the mainland of Asia. It faces the Soviet Union, North and South Korea, and China. More than 95 percent of the Japanese population live on four large islands, Hokkaido, Honshu, Kyushu, and Shikoku, which stretch 1,200 miles along the east coast of the Asian continent. Okinawa lies another 600 miles to the southeast and there are thousands of smaller islands. Northern Hokkaido is at the latitude of Minneapolis, Minnesota, and Okinawa is at the latitude of Miami, Florida, making the distance between Japan's northern and southern extremities almost as great as that of the continental United States. The

Japan Information Center, Consulate General of Japan

The climate in Japan is generally mild and the four seasons are clearly distinctive. Spring is the glory of the year with balmy days and bright sunshine. Spring also brings the cherry blossom with all its delicate fragrance. Cherry blossoms are found in all parts of the country. Lake Yamanaka pictured here is one of the noted places for viewing the cherry blossoms and world-famous Mt. Fuji.

widest point east to west is 120 miles, and much of the land is narrower.

It is never more than 50 miles to the sea from any location

in Japan and it is rarely more than 50 miles to a mountain. Those two facts explain much of the love of the Japanese for both sea and mountains, a love shared by many Japanese Americans as well. The symbol of Japan is Mount Fuji, always repectfully addressed as Fuji-san to indicate its importance (the honorific "san" is customarily used to address one's human superiors). The perpetually snowcapped mountain rises to 12,388 feet above sea level and is the highest mountain in the highest range—the Japanese Alps. An active volcano located about 80 miles southeast of Tokyo, Mount Fuji was visible from Tokyo on almost any clear day until increased air pollution obscured the view. It is the desire of all Japanese to make a pilgrimage to climb Mount Fuji, and the great majority do so at least once in their life. There are stations allowing rest and overnight stops on the way.

Although the islands are mountainous, most Japanese live on the plains. Approximately 20 percent of the land area of Japan is relatively flat. The largest such region is the Kanto Plain, on which Tokyo is located. In the plains virtually every foot of land is used either for agriculture, industry, or housing. In contrast, it is often possible to walk for miles through the mountains without meeting any human inhabitants. Consequently, one of the great good fortunes of Japan is that much of its landscape today greatly resembles its appearance in woodblock prints made four centuries ago.

The climate varies widely throughout Japan. In 1964, the Winter Olympics were held in Sapporo, the largest city on the northern island of Hokkaido, which is very cold and snowy every winter. To the south, Okinawa has a tropical climate with date palms and pineapples in abundance. Even cities such as Fukuoka and Nagasaki on Kyushu are very humid and often have temperatures above 100 degrees in the summer. Cities in central Japan are generally moderate in climate, with Tokyo averaging 86 degrees for the high in August and 30

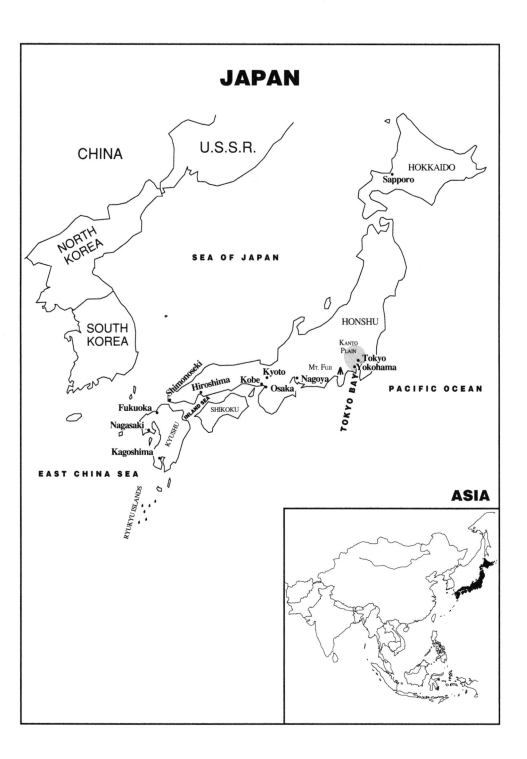

JAPAN

CHINA

U.S.S.R.

HOKKAIDO

Sapporo

NORTH KOREA

SEA OF JAPAN

SOUTH KOREA

HONSHU

KANTO PLAIN

MT. FUJI

Tokyo

Yokohama

Shimonoseki

Hiroshima

Kobe

Kyoto

Nagoya

Osaka

PACIFIC OCEAN

TOKYO BAY

Fukuoka

INLAND SEA

SHIKOKU

Nagasaki

KYUSHU

Kagoshima

EAST CHINA SEA

RYUKYU ISLANDS

ASIA

degrees for the low in January and February. Rainfall is abundant throughout the country, with almost every area receiving more than 40 inches a year. Several typhoons, or Pacific hurricanes, strike the Japanese islands each year in the late summer and early fall, bringing intense rain, high winds, and destruction to houses and crops.

THE PEOPLE OF JAPAN

Approximately 124 million people live in Japan as of 1990, making it the world's seventh largest country in population behind China, India, the Soviet Union, the United States, Indonesia, and Germany. Its population density of 850 per square mile is second only to The Netherlands. With 8.25 million people, Tokyo is the third largest city in the world, with the greater Tokyo metropolitan area containing about 17 million people. According to the 1985 Japanese census, there were eleven cities with populations greater than one million. Because Japan's populated areas are overcrowded, one of the great attractions for Japanese emigrating to other countries has been space. Consequently, the United States, Canada, and Brazil have been the most common destinations for Japanese emigrants.

The original inhabitants of Japan were a people called the Ainu, approximately 15,000 of whom still reside in Hokkaido. They are very closely related to the Indians of the American Northwest and British Columbia in Canada. Apparently, the Ainu turned south to Japan as the Indians continued northeast to Alaska and America approximately 15,000 years ago. However, by 4500 B.C. groups of Asian peoples began to arrive in Japan, migrating from China to Korea to Kyushu, the main southwestern island. They spread steadily northward, taking over the entire country. Today the Japanese are one of the world's most homogeneous peoples, possessing very similar racial and linguistic characteristics. Less than 1 million of the 124 million inhabitants of Japan are Korean, Chinese, Ainu, or members of other ethnic groups.

Population grew at a moderate rate until about 1870, when there were 30 million Japanese. By 1970, the population had soared to more than 110 million. Since then the growth has been quite slow because of a low birth rate, averaging only 1 percent growth a year. Before World War II, the ideal Japanese family consisted of four to eight children, but now the ideal family has two children. Boys have always been the preferred children since the society is patriarchal, with inheritance through the male side of the family. The oldest son is obligated to support the parents and maintain the altar to the spirits of departed ancestors.

THE HISTORY OF JAPAN

Traditionally, Japanese history has been divided into fifteen periods called *Jidai* (Gee•day) covering about 200 years each. Early Japanese history consists of tribal groups competing with each other. By the fourth century A.D., Japan was unified under the leadership of the Yamato court, which established a centralized government at Dazaifu in Kyushu. The Heian era began in A.D. 794, when the emperor Kammu completed building of the new capital at Heian (present-day Kyoto) and developed a central government, modeled after the Chinese bureaucratic system. Though the political leadership of the country shifted to Tokyo in the nineteenth century, Kyoto remains the philosophical, religious, and cultural center of Japan.

The Fujiwaras, a great noble family, gained power over the emperor in A.D. 852. During the three-hundred-year Fujiwara period, this family maintained control through their positions as imperial regents and councillors. What emerged in Japan was a feudal system in which economic power was in the hands of the daimyo, or great landlords, who hired bands of

professional warriors called samurai to protect themselves and
the peasants who worked the land. The military influence of
these samurai increased, and in 1192 a samurai named
Yoritomo was named as shogun (general) to protect the
emperor. In their position as military regents, the Kamakura
shoguns controlled the emperor and ruled in his name. From
1192 through 1867, a series of shogun families governed Japan
through their military might.

In 1336 a samurai leader named Takauji Ashikaga gained
control of Kyoto; his family ruled Japan for 225 years. It was
during the later part of the Ashikaga era that the Portuguese
became the first Europeans to reach Japan. Initially Portuguese
traders and the Christian missionaries who came with them
were welcomed in Japan, particularly in the south. The Jesuits,
led by Saint Francis Xavier in 1549, established a strong
presence and spread Christianity throughout the kingdom. In
1585 a great warrior named Hideyoshi gained control in Japan.
He invaded Korea twice and conceived of a great Japanese
overseas empire. After his death, a new era called Edo began
in 1603 with the accession to power of Ieyasu Tokugawa. The
Tokugawas moved the capital to Edo (modern Tokyo) and
ruled the country for more than 250 years. By 1630 the family
had decided that contact with the outside world was
dangerous. They expelled all the Christian missionaries from
Japan and, except for a few secret believers, forced all
Japanese to give up Christianity. Foreign sailors shipwrecked
in Japan were executed. Japanese citizens were not allowed to
travel abroad and Japanese living abroad were not allowed to
return to Japan. The only outside contact allowed in the
isolated kingdom was one Dutch ship a year allowed at a
small island in the harbor at Nagasaki. During the Tokugawa
period, Japanese culture acquired many of its most distinctive
features.

By the early 1800's the United States was conducting trade

A U.S. ship in a Japanese harbor is depicted here as trade relations began in the mid-1800's.

with China and wished to open trade relations with Japan as well. In addition, the United States was concerned about the treatment of shipwrecked American sailors in Japan and wanted to establish diplomatic ties in order to remedy the situation. On July 8, 1853, Commodore Matthew C. Perry sailed four American ships into Tokyo harbor and presented American demands for open diplomatic and trade relations. Negotiations led to the Treaty of Kanagawa in 1854 and several treaties were signed between Japan and the United States, Great Britain, The Netherlands, and Russia which allowed trade in special ports and established the principle of extraterritoriality (the right to have their citizens subject to their nation's own laws rather than those of Japan).

These treaties greatly displeased many daimyo from western Japan. In 1867 they overthrew the Tokugawas and restored the emperor Mutsuhito to power, beginning the Meiji period in Japan. This period was one of rapid modernization and adaptation to foreign influences, particularly that of the United States. Education became compulsory and thousands of schools were established. The samurai were abolished and a modern army and navy were established. The government encouraged industrialization and brought in many Western experts to assist them. By 1920 the economic system was dominated by Zaibatsu—huge corporations controlled by single families which operated the larger banks, factories, mines, and trading companies. In 1889 the Meiji Constitution established a two-house parliament called the Diet and a modern bureaucracy to run the country. By then Japan had an eye toward expanding its influence in Asia. During wars with China in 1894-1895 and Russia in 1904-1905, Japan acquired control of Taiwan, dominance in Korea, and numerous rights in Manchuria. Fighting on the Allied side in World War I led to the acquisition of the Mariana, Caroline, and Marshall islands of the western Pacific and the German trading rights in

Shandong province in China.

During the 1920's Japan developed her overseas trade. The depression of the 1930's and the growing strength of China provided a rationale for the seizure of increasing power by the Japanese military. The first result was the occupation of the Manchurian peninsula in 1931, followed by the invasion of the Chinese mainland in 1937. On December 7, 1941, Japanese naval forces struck the American naval base at Pearl Harbor in Hawaii and the Pacific War (World War II) began. Despite their early successes, the Japanese were overwhelmed by the Allied forces, principally the United States, China, Great Britain, Australia, New Zealand, and Canada. At the end of World War II the Japanese economy was shattered, all of the major cities except Kyoto were in ruins, millions of soldiers and civilians had been killed, and the nation was starving. By the terms of the surrender treaty, Japan lost all of its land except the four main islands and several smaller ones nearby. At the same time Emperor Hirohito renounced his claims to divinity and accepted a position as the symbolic head of state.

Actual political power was transferred in August, 1945, to General Douglas MacArthur of the United States who headed the Allied military occupation of Japan. In 1947, the occupation forces imposed the modern Japanese Constitution whose provisions abolished the armed forces and have allowed only a small self-defense force. Real political power is now in the hands of the Liberal Democratic Party, which has dominated the Diet since its establishment out of two earlier parties in the early 1950's. On April 28, 1952, the United State and Japan signed a peace treaty ending American occupation of Japan.

The story of Japan in the last forty years is that of an almost miraculous economic recovery made after the war until the country now is one of the three major economic powers in the world along with Western Europe and the United States.

That recovery seems based on the importation at low cost of the modern technology of the West, on an educated and dedicated work force, and on great self-discipline that sees most families save up to 15 percent of their income every year.

JAPAN TODAY

When modernization began in the late nineteenth century, Japan's economy was overwhelmingly rural. Since nearly 75 percent of the land was unsuitable for crops, the farms were tiny in comparison to farms in the United States. The average size of the modern Japanese farm, 2.2 acres, is about the same as it was a century ago. Furthermore, each farm family had several small fields—about one-eighth of an acre in size—scattered around the village, rather than a single large holding. As a result, Japanese farmers relied on intensive hand-tilled cultivation and large amounts of fertilizer to produce high yields of rice and various vegetables. They maintained few livestock other than the oxen used for plowing and pulling carts and some chickens raised for their eggs and meat. A related occupation for many farmers near the seashore was fishing, and fish provided another primary source of meat in Japan. A major change in Japanese agriculture occurred after World War II when occupation forces transferred ownership of the land from the daimyo to the farmers themselves. Although the economic situation of the farmers improved, the percentage of Japanese farmers has declined dramatically during the last thirty years as the nation has industrialized even further.

During the early period of industrialization, Japanese products were considered cheap and poorly made, and the postwar industrial boom did not immediately change this reputation. Since then, however, modern Japanese automobiles, electronic equipment, cameras, watches, and other products have become synonymous with extremely high quality. Many Japanese industrial firms are large publicly owned corporations where loyal employees work during their entire careers. Decisions are made in group consultation and then are followed with great dedication. Many Japanese are commonly identified by their place of employment, such as Sato-san of Suzuki (Mr. Sato who works for Suzuki). The success of these Japanese corporations has led to the creation of American-based subsidiaries. Among those prominent in the United States today are Nissan, Honda, Toyota, Bridgestone, Sony, Sharp, Toshiba, and Hitachi.

The Japanese have also become prominent in the financial industry. Because the Japanese save a very high percentage of their income, Japanese banks and industrial concerns have become financial leaders in the Pacific Rim region and have great influence in the world economy as well. These banks and corporations have acquired large amounts of land, buildings, and companies in other countries, especially in the United States. Many of the leading Japanese banks, including Sanwa, Mitsui Manufacturers, Sumitomo, and Tokai, have branches in American cities.

WHY AMERICA?

The first Japanese to immigrate to the United States came to Hawaii in 1868, the first year of the reign of the Emperor Meiji. They called themselves *Gannen Mono*, "first-year men." They came to Hawaii on three-year contracts to work on the sugarcane plantations. These laborers came primarily from the Hiroshima, Kumamoto, Wakayama, Fukuoka, and Yamaguchi provinces of western Japan. Though they were from farm families, these workers had the equivalent of an eighth-grade education, which was far above the average for the United States at the time. In fact, these laborers for the most part were middle-class males whose chief aim was to earn enough money to return to Japan and purchase land. They found the plantation work extremely hard and complained to the Japanese government. When their contracts were finished in 1871, many of these laborers went back to Japan, but some stayed in Hawaii permanently.

Meanwhile in 1869, John Henry Schnell led a group of immigrants from Wakamatsu to California to try to establish tea and silkworm culture. They settled at Gold Hill, near Sacramento, but the colony failed and dissolved by 1871. One grave remains to give evidence of their presence. Its inscription reads, "In memory of Okei/ Died in 1871/ Age 19 years/ A Japanese girl."

SEEKING AN AMERICAN EDUCATION

During the 1860's and 1870's, a small number of young boys and a handful of young girls were sent to the United States to gain the benefits of a Western education. Japan had emerged from nearly two centuries of self-imposed isolation with the realization that it would have to transform itself from a rural society with an economy based primarily on farming and fishing to a modern industrial economy able to produce coal, silk fabric, paper, tea, and other manufactured goods that could be traded with the West. Japanese citizens with firsthand knowledge of Western methods would become an asset in this push to achieve economic equality with Western nations.

These student visitors from Japan were members of the upper class. The U.S. census for 1880 showed 148 students attending colleges and universities, primarily in the East and Midwest. The number of Japanese student visitors rapidly increased after 1885 when new laws made it much easier for the Japanese to leave their home country.

Finding the money to study in America was very difficult for those individuals without wealthy families or government funding to support them. Many of these Japanese students took part-time employment as domestic servants in exchange for room and board and a small wage. Although their work often left them with little time for their studies, these Japanese student workers did gain a great deal of practical knowledge of American culture as a result of their experiences. Most of these early students went back to Japan, but some, like Onuki Hachiro (or Hutchlon Ohnick), stayed. He began companies in Phoenix to produce illuminating gas and also electricity. These two companies were later combined to become the Arizona Public Service Company.

THE EXODUS TO HAWAII

Japan's push for industrialization took its toll on Japanese farmers. Faced with high taxes and economic policies that decreased the value of their rice crops, many farmers lost their land or were forced to sell all of it to pay their debts. One way for Japanese families to earn the money to purchase back these farms was to hire themselves out as contract laborers to work on the sugarcane and pineapple plantations of Hawaii. The first laborers who left Japan in 1868 were secretly recruited, but beginning in 1884 the Japanese government officially authorized recruitment of contract laborers by Hawaiian plantation owners. Two shiploads of contract laborers left for Hawaii in 1885 and by 1894, 28,691 had come. The great majority of these laborers were single men who planned to make money quickly and return to Japan, but only about 7,500 actually returned. Most Japanese plantation laborers stayed and became American residents when the United States acquired Hawaii as a territory in 1898. Their children became the first Nisei and the first Japanese-American citizens.

LABORING ON THE MAINLAND

Beginning in the 1890's, Japanese laborers were migrating to the United States to fill positions that became available after the Chinese Exclusion Act of 1882 prohibited further immigration of Chinese laborers. The demand for labor on the West Coast led to a rapid increase of Japanese immigration both from Japan and Hawaii. The early Japanese in California found employment as railroads laborers, cannery employees, loggers, miners, meatpackers, farm workers, and domestic servants. They worked hard for wages that ranged between $1 and $1.50 per day and endured harsh conditions. Although these wages were low by American standards, they were very attractive to Japanese immigrants struggling to earn the funds to return home as prosperous citizens. A secondary region offering jobs for the Japanese was the state of Washington, where both the Great Northern and Northern Pacific railroads needed construction laborers. By 1900 some 22,000 Japanese lived in California and 3,000 lived in Washington state.

New arrivals at Angel Island Immigration Station, California.

THE PICTURE BRIDES

As time passed, many Japanese male immigrants were choosing to stay in the United States. Some had left families in Japan, but others were reaching the age where they began to consider starting families. Anti-Asian feeling, including laws forbidding interracial marriages, made it necessary for these men to look for Japanese brides. Many preferred to have a wife who would understand their language and heritage.

43

The solution to this problem was "picture brides." Traditionally, Japanese marriages had been arranged by matchmakers, though the bride and groom usually knew each other. Now Japanese-American men sent their pictures to matchmakers in Japan, who arranged with the young women's families for marriages. The matchmakers tried to pair the men with women who shared similar family backgrounds, and tried to match couples who came from the same ken ("state") and even the same village or town in Japan if possible. Strong young women who could bear several children were preferred, and most were younger daughters of large families. The proposed bride's picture was sent to the man, and if he agreed, the marriage was arranged. Usually the marriage ceremony was performed by proxy—a brother, cousin, or other male relative would serve as a stand-in for the groom—and the bride would not meet her husband until she arrived in America.

Between 1908 and 1924, when Japanese immigration was halted, 66,926 Japanese women entered Hawaii and the mainland. Although some were plantation laborers, most arrived as picture brides. These women outnumbered male immigrants during the period by 2 to 1. This was in great contrast to the period before 1908, when males outnumbered females by 6 to 1.

OPPORTUNITIES IN CANADA

In 1886, the first Japanese reached Victoria, British Columbia, Canada. The Canadian provinces offered many of the same employment opportunities found in the United States. By 1901 there were 4,700 Japanese immigrants residing in Canada. They were almost all males and worked in gangs on the railways and roads or in mining and lumbering. Later they would switch to farming and fishing. Although these laborers often migrated from region to region seeking jobs, most of the

Japanese immigrants lived in British Columbia, many in "Little Tokyo" in Vancouver. Some of the Canadian citizens of British Columbia tried to convince their legislators to alter the 1923 immigration law which excluded Chinese so that it would apply to the Japanese. Though these efforts failed to exclude the Japanese, very few immigrants came during the 1930's.

WHEN THEY CAME

As is the case for other immigrant groups who came to North America, Japanese immigrants arrived in large numbers during the early years and then immigration tapered off dramatically (see tables). Several factors account for this pattern of arrival.

STRANGERS FROM THE EAST

Although the number of Japanese students and laborers who first emigrated to Hawaii and the United States in the late 1860's was quite small, the Japanese became the largest Asian group in the United States by 1910, with more than 73,000 residents on the mainland and nearly 80,000 residents in the U.S. territory of Hawaii (see table on the following page). The passage of the Chinese Exclusion Act in 1882 combined with the lifting of a Japanese imperial ban on emigration in 1886 to produce a flood of Japanese immigrants to Hawaii and the United States. Japanese immigrants arrived in Canada slightly later. In 1907 alone, more than 8,000 Japanese laborers arrived in British Columbia seeking work in the canning and logging industries.

Japanese immigration peaked in the decade from 1900 to 1910, when 125,000 Japanese arrived in the United States and Hawaii. In March, 1907, President Theodore Roosevelt issued an order barring Japanese immigration into the continental United States from Canada, Mexico, or the Hawaiian Territory. Then by a series of diplomatic notes in 1907-1908, the Gentlemen's Agreement was developed. Japan made a major concession to the United States by agreeing to cease issuing

JAPANESE POPULATION IN THE UNITED STATES
AND HAWAII, 1890-1990

Year	Japanese population	In Hawaii	On U.S. mainland
1890	14,000	12,000	2,000
1900	85,716	61,111	24,605
1910	191,009	79,675	73,070
1920	220,596	109,274	111,322
1930	278,743	139,631	139,112
1940	285,115	157,905	127,210
1950	326,379	184,611	141,768
1960	464,332	203,455	260,877
1970	591,290	217,175	374,115
1980	716,331	239,738	476,593
1990*	800,000+	—	—

Sources: Population Reference Bureau, Inc.; *The New York Times.*
*Note: Exact data from 1990 census not available.

passports to skilled and unskilled laborers. However, students, businessmen, and the parents, wives, and children of laborers already in the United States could still come. The result was a dramatic drop in Japanese immigration, from 30,824 in 1907 to 3,275 in 1909.

During the 1920's, only 85,000 additional immigrants arrived from Japan. This decrease was due, in part, to effects of the Gentlemen's Agreement. In 1921, the Japanese government ceased issuing passports to picture brides, but this did not satisfy the Japanese Exclusion League and other opponents of Japanese immigration. The passage of the Immigration Act of 1924 prohibited the immigration of all aliens ineligible for citizenship, a category which included the Japanese. With the ending of Japanese immigration, the relationship between Japan and the United States began to worsen noticeably, eventually bringing the two countries into conflict during World War II.

RESTRICTIVE LEGISLATION

In California the fear of a "yellow peril" led to further problems for the Japanese. In particular, there was now a fear that the Japanese would purchase large amounts of farm land. Consequently, in 1913 and again in 1920 California passed laws making "aliens ineligible for citizenship" unable to purchase land and allowing three-year leases at maximum. These Alien Land Laws, which applied only to Chinese, Japanese, and other Asians, did have one major loophole. A Japanese family could purchase land in the name of a citizen child and then serve as that child's guardian. Many families did that and avoided losing their farm land. Similar laws followed in Washington, Oregon, Idaho, Arizona, New Mexico, Nevada, Texas, and Nebraska.

On the West Coast, William Randolph Hearst and his newspapers and V. S. McClatchy, head of the Japanese Exclusion League, led a determined effort for many years to end Japanese immigration into the United States. Finally, Congress took up a new immigration bill in 1924. The House of Representatives excluded "aliens ineligible for citizenship" from immigrating to the United States but the Senate seemed inclined to allow up to 100 Japanese a year to come to the United States. However, late in the Senate debate Senator Henry Cabot Lodge of Massachusetts came to support exclusion, and this was adopted as the law of the country in 1924.

A MODEST INCREASE

The worldwide economic troubles of the 1930's and World War II in the 1940's effectively diminished Japanese immigration to its lowest levels (see table). Postwar prosperity and the passage of the Soldier's Bride Act in 1947 were responsible for the increase to 46,000 during the period from 1951 to 1960. In the period after 1965, Asian immigration

JAPANESE IMMIGRATION TO THE UNITED STATES
AND HAWAII, 1890-1990

Year(s)	New immigrants
1890	2,000
1891-1900	30,000
1901-1910	125,000
1911-1920	85,000
1921-1930	33,000
1931-1940	2,000
1941-1950	2,000
1951-1960	46,000
1961-1970	41,000
1971-1980	49,000
1981-1990	42,000
Total	457,000

Sources: Tricia Knoll, *Becoming Americans: Asian Sojourners, Immigrants, and Refugees in the Western United States* (Portland, Ore.: Coast to Coast Books, 1982), pp. 308-309; Population Reference Bureau, Inc.

quotas were lifted and large numbers of Chinese, Vietnamese, Laotians, and Filipinos came to the United States. This change in immigration law did not lead to large numbers of Japanese permanent residents. Approximately 4,000 have migrated to the United States each year since 1965. The small number of Japanese coming yearly to the United States is primarily related to the great economic growth of Japan, where excellent jobs and living conditions encourage most Japanese to remain. The total of 100,000 new Japanese Americans in the twenty-five years from 1965 to 1990 represents one-eighth of the total of Japanese Americans counted in the 1990 census. Further they represent a major younger element among an aging overall population.

CANADA: ANOTHER OPTION

The Japanese began to enter British Columbia on Canada's West Coast in 1886 and by 1900 there were some 17,000 there. Their experience paralleled the experiences of the Japanese Americans on the West Coast of the United States, including relocation during World War II from the coastal areas of British Columbia where virtually all lived. After the war, extreme discrimination continued in British Columbia for a few years and some 4,000 Japanese Canadians went back to Japan. The great majority relocated elsewhere in Canada. Today, about 41,000 live in Canada, with some 16,000 each in Ontario and in inland British Columbia and the others widely scattered. Generally, the Nisei and Sansei in Canada have been assimilated into the larger Canadian society. Economically, the Japanese Canadian is now equal to other Canadians and discrimination has largely disappeared.

WHERE THEY LIVE

In the period since 1965, changes have occurred in the living patterns of Asians in North America. New immigration laws in the United States and Canada admitted large numbers of Chinese, Vietnamese, Laotians, Filipinos, and other Asian groups. For much of their history, Asian Americans have been concentrated geographically on the West Coast of the United States and Canada. According to the 1980 U.S. Census, 56 percent of all Asian Americans lived in the West; preliminary figures for 1990 show an increase to 58 percent. At the same time, the Asian-American population is dispersing into other regions. Asian-American population figures for 1990 show three East Coast states—New York, Illinois, and New Jersey— ranked ahead of western states such as Washington and Texas. While the majority are still West Coast residents, Japanese Americans have contributed to this trend of geographic dispersal.

GO EAST, YOUNG MAN

At the end of World War II, the great majority of Japanese Americans returned to their former homes in Hawaii and on the West Coast. As illustrated in the table below, 37.5 percent of the Japanese population in the United States in 1980 lived in California, 33.5 percent lived in Hawaii, and 3.8 percent lived in the state of Washington, which has the third largest Japanese-American population. Only 29 percent of the entire Japanese-American population lived in the rest of the United States. Another characteristic of the Japanese-American population is that almost all live in urban, as opposed to rural,

JAPANESE-AMERICAN POPULATION
BY STATE AND CITY, 1980

Area/City	Population	Foreign-Born	American-born
California	268,814		
Los Angeles/Long Beach	117,190	33,381	83,809
San Francisco/Oakland	40,390	13,126	27,264
San Jose	22,262	4,876	17,386
Anaheim/Santa Ana	21,841	6,066	15,775
Sacramento	14,836	2,994	11,842
San Diego	13,110	5,828	7,282
Hawaii	239,734		
Honolulu	190,218	19,074	171,144
Washington	27,389		
Seattle	17,952	5,057	12,895
New York	24,754		
New York City	23,241	17,930	5,311
Illinois	18,432		
Chicago	16,042	6,229	9,813
Other states	137,204		
Total	716,331	(203,338)	(523,993)

Source: U.S. Department of Commerce, *1980 Census of Population: Asian and Pacific Islander Population.*

areas. According to the 1980 census, 636,621 out of 716,331 Japanese in America lived in Standard Metropolitan statistical areas (SMSAs), and most of the other 79,710 lived in smaller urban areas. Eight of the ten largest urban concentrations of Japanese-American population are on the Pacific Coast (see table above). It is interesting to note that New York City is ranked fourth and Chicago is ranked eighth among these cities.

The Japanese population living outside Hawaii, California, Oregon, and Washington represents a major shift in the living patterns for Japanese Americans. Less than 5 percent of the population in 1940, 14 percent in 1960, and 19 percent in 1970 lived outside of these Pacific Coast states. It is expected

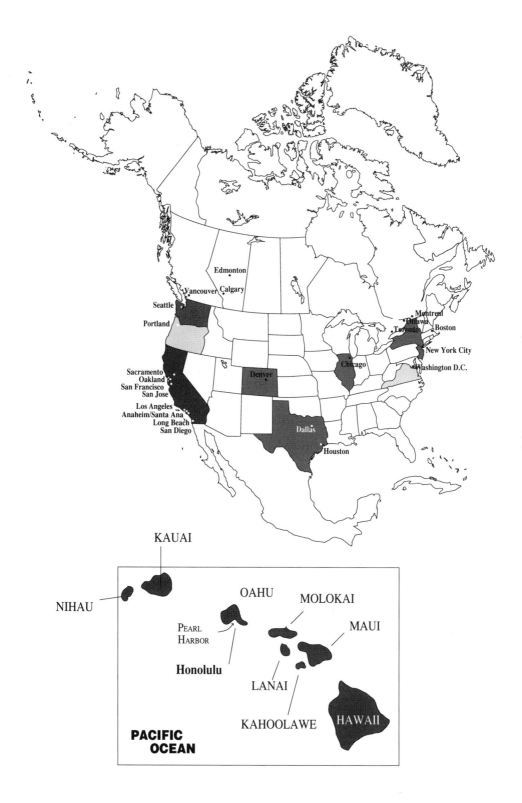

Edmonton

Vancouver Calgary

Seattle

Portland

Sacramento
Oakland
San Francisco
San Jose

Los Angeles
Anaheim/Santa Ana
Long Beach
San Diego

Denver

Dallas

Houston

Chicago

Montreal
Ottawa
Toronto
Boston

New York City

Washington D.C.

KAUAI

NIHAU

OAHU

MOLOKAI

PEARL
HARBOR

MAUI

Honolulu

LANAI

KAHOOLAWE

HAWAII

PACIFIC
OCEAN

that this trend will continue and further dispersal of the population will occur.

Several reasons account for this change. First, the Nisei who left the camps in 1943-1944 to work in war industries and other occupations were required to move to the East and Midwest, where many of them remained after the war. Second, it became the perception of many Japanese Americans that economic and social opportunities were better in these areas where anti-Asian prejudice was not so prevalent. As one Denver newspaper editor said, "I'm almost certain that a major Los Angeles or San Francisco newspaper would not appoint me to this position."

The same trend of outmigration can be seen in Hawaii. Although the total Japanese population in Hawaii continues to grow, the percentage has steadily declined since 1930. This change has occurred because large numbers of people from other ethnic groups are moving to the islands from the mainland. At the same time, many Japanese Americans—who make up the majority of students at the University of Hawaii—find employment on the mainland and leave Hawaii. In 1970 the Japanese were replaced by Caucasians as the largest single group in the islands for the first time since the 1890's. Second in the overall population, they are still the largest ethnic minority group, possessing tremendous economic and political power.

THE KAI-SHA

Beginning in the 1960's Japanese immigrants of a new type have come to the United States. These are the kai-sha, representatives of large Japanese industrial and trading corporations. Some of the kai-sha are temporary residents; they come for several months or a few years until their corporations send them back to Japan. Other kai-sha have become permanent residents. As a result, urban centers where kai-sha work—cities such as New York City, San Diego, Chicago, San Francisco, and Los Angeles—have more Japanese-born residents than the American average. Many of the kai-sha have such an excellent command of English and a fine understanding of American business that their companies find them too valuable to be brought back to Japan.

Beginning about 1975, some Japanese industrial firms have sent managers to head up corporate divisions in the United States. These kai-sha are responsible for supervising the work of American employees. Originally, most of these companies were concentrated in California, which still retains a slight lead over other states. However, since 1980, there has been a major shift to the southeastern United States, an area with few Japanese Americans. During his tenure as governor of Tennessee, Lamar Alexander (now the U.S. secretary of education) was instrumental in attracting Japanese corporations to this region, and he became one of the best known Americans in Japan because of his industrial promotion tours. Tennessee, now second to California, has some 96 Japanese firms in operation within the state, including the main manufacturing facilities of Nissan automobiles and Bridgestone tires. Though many of these firms are located in Memphis and Nashville, others are found in towns as small as Livingston, Mt. Pleasant, and Vonore, all having populations of less than 3,000. This industrialization is also a major factor in such states as Kentucky, Arkansas, and Alabama.

WHAT THEY DO

The occupations held by members of the Japanese-American community have always reflected their industriousness as well as their diversity as individuals. As seen in earlier chapters, the first Japanese immigrants to North America worked in a variety of labor-intensive, low-paying jobs. The Japanese-American community in the 1990's includes individuals from nearly every field of employment imaginable: from deli owners to investment bankers, from mail carriers to musicians, and from farmers to physicists. The shift from menial day laborers to successful professionals did not occur overnight. Americans and Canadians of Japanese descent struggled for many decades to overcome the racial prejudices which prevented them from pursuing the kinds of careers for which their education had prepared them.

THE EARLY WORKERS

As discussed in earlier chapters, many of the Japanese immigrants who first arrived in North America worked as laborers. Since most unions refused to admit Asians as members, Japanese laborers were forced to accept the lowest paying positions and to endure harsh conditions that union laborers did not face. For some Japanese immigrants, their experiences as farmers and fishermen provided them with the skills necessary to plant and harvest crops and to catch and process fish. Others were active in railroad construction, logging, and factory jobs that became available after Chinese immigration was halted in 1882.

Some Japanese immigrants found employment in American

cities. In San Francisco in 1906 there were 10,000 Japanese
workers. Almost 3,000 were domestic workers, 1,500 ran
hotels or boarding houses, and nearly 1,000 worked for
Caucasian-owned stores. Some Issei workers were able to save
enough of their wages to establish their own small businesses.
There were many self-employed Japanese working as barbers,
laundry owners, bookstore owners, curio dealers, bath house
owners, pool hall operators, watch repairmen, and so forth.
Many of these businesses—hotels, boarding houses, tailor
shops, markets, and dry goods stores—provided services for
the growing Japanese communities. It was common practice
for Japanese entrepreneurs to hire other Japanese workers,
mostly from their own provinces or towns in Japan. Though
wages were low, this practice of ethnic solidarity provide
many Japanese workers with job security during times of
difficulty, such as the Great Depression of the 1930's, since
Japanese tradition encouraged employers to retain all workers
in recognition of their mutual dependence and kinship
obligations.

Others decided to channel their efforts into establishing their
own farms. Most of the land they used was leased from
others, though some Japanese had managed to purchase their
own land. By 1921, Japanese farmers were producing 12.3
percent of all crops in California, especially emphasizing rice
and potatoes. Although some of these farms produced food to
support the Japanese themselves, other farms were large
enough and successful enough to compete for a share of the
larger agricultural market. Owners of these large farm
operations—such as George Shima, the "Potato King" of the
Sacramento River valley—hired other Japanese workers who
were eager to prove their worth.

SURVIVING THE DEPRESSION

Like other Americans, the Japanese found the depression

Japanese-American farmworker in Nyssa, Oregon, 1942.

years of the 1930's economically difficult. In California, however, they continued to be successful in agriculture. Japanese Americans had become heavily involved in truck farming, raising fresh vegetables and fruit for sale in the towns. By 1940, they produced more than 90 percent of the snap beans, celery, peppers, and strawberries; more than half of the artichokes, cauliflower, cucumbers, spinach, and tomatoes; and more than 25 percent of the asparagus, cantaloupes, carrots, lettuce, onions and watermelons. Many Japanese Americans were involved in a related occupation: gardening. These gardeners took care of lawns, hedges, plants, and trees for wealthy homeowners in Hollywood, Los Angeles, Berkeley, and Oakland. There were some 1,800 independent Japanese gardening firms in Southern California alone by 1940, and the gardener as a skilled businessman was often the most independent-minded of all Japanese Americans.

By the 1930 census, there were 139,631 Japanese Americans in Hawaii, 38 percent of the total population. They were by far the largest single group in a multi-ethnic population. By that time, many Nisei had become physicians, dentists, schoolteachers, government administrators, and businessmen, as well as workers in white-owned establishments. Though some hostility existed and political control remained in the hands of a white minority, discrimination was not very serious, in contrast to the mainland.

THE MODEL MINORITY

Economically, Japanese Americans have changed since World War II from a laboring group to a more prosperous managerial and professional group. In 1986, *Newsweek* labeled Asian Americans "A Model Minority," *Fortune* called them "America's Super Minority," and *The New Republic* extolled their success as "America's greatest success story." That same year Asian Americans were featured on the *NBC Nightly*

News, on *60 Minutes*, and on the *McNeil/Lehrer Report*.
Although many Japanese and other Asian Americans feel that
this new stereotype of ethnic success is no more flattering or
accurate than previous Asian stereotypes, the label "model
minority" does call attention to their achievements in America.

Why have modern Japanese Americans been considered so
successful? In 1978, Darrel Montero, a professor of sociology
at the University of California, Los Angeles (UCLA), listed
two reasons. (1) Japanese Americans have the highest average
educational level of any group in America and (2) Japanese
Americans are twice as likely to be employed as professionals
as members of society as a whole. Certainly, the strong
emphasis on education is part of the perception of Japanese
Americans as a model minority. As for the second factor,
median family income in 1980 was $27,354, almost 40 percent
above the national average and second only to the Jewish
Americans among identifiable ethnic groups.

EDUCATION: THE KEY TO EMPLOYMENT

For Japanese Americans in the United States and Canada,
higher education is closely linked to economic opportunities.
Eighty-eight percent of all Japanese-American students now go
on to college. The numbers of Japanese and other Asian
Americans scoring high on the SAT and ACT college entrance
tests has led to unofficial maximum quotas at the Berkeley and
Los Angeles campuses of the University of California. Even
so, in the fall of 1990, UCLA admitted more Asian-American
freshmen than Caucasians for the first time, and Japanese
Americans were a great part of that success. California State
University, Los Angeles, and the private University of
Southern California both have a large Asian-American
presence on campus and have admitted all qualified students.
These institutions of higher education have graduated 8,000
engineers, 3,400 medical doctors, and 7,000 teachers,

A stellar example of the commitment to education, Lucy Shigemitsu, of New York, was a finalist in the 48th Annual Science Talent Search (STS) sponsored by the Westinghouse Electric Corporation and Science Service. She chose a cancer research study for her project.

indicating that such occupations are now open to all qualified persons.

Studies of Japanese-American college students do reveal certain career interests. A survey of Japanese-American males attending California State University, Sacramento, in the 1970's showed that most were majoring in business (37 percent) and the sciences (26 percent), with a scattering in other majors. In 1979 at the University of Hawaii, Japanese-American undergraduates (40 percent of the undergraduate enrollment) tended to concentrate on education, engineering, and human resource majors, with business administration only slightly behind. Japanese-American masters and doctoral students (21 percent and 16 percent, respectively, of the graduate totals) concentrated on advanced degrees in education, law, and medicine. Similar studies in 1980 at the University of British Columbia showed a preference for majors in education and physical education, followed by the biological sciences, business, and the social sciences.

EMPLOYMENT OPPORTUNITIES TODAY

Japanese Americans have increasingly turned from the original farming occupations of the Issei to more professional jobs. However, the ones who have remained in agriculture, primarily in Hawaii and California, have often done well financially. In 1970 in Hawaii the U.S. census showed the following major occupations for Japanese Americans.

In 1974, 69 percent of all teachers in Hawaii's school systems were Japanese Americans as well as 28 percent of the school administrators and 70 percent of the school board members. As early as the 1960 census Japanese Americans were heavily represented nationwide among dentists (especially in Hawaii, where they made up 60 percent of the total), architects, artists and writers, natural scientists, and technicians. They were well represented among physicians,

OCCUPATIONS OF JAPANESE AMERICANS IN
HAWAII, 1970

Occupations	Male	Female
Craftsmen and Foremen	17,654	835
Professional/Technical	8,156	7,425
Managerial/Administrative	7,528	2,036
Operators/Transport Workers	6,672	4,645
Clerical	5,648	16,200
Service Workers	3,912	9,191
Laborers	3,751	312
Sales	3,527	4,251
Farm Laborers	1,075	548
Farm Owners/Managers	715	314
Private Household Workers	20	1,081

Source: Harry H. L. Kitano, *Japanese Americans: The Evolution of a Subculture.*
2d ed. (Englewood Cliffs, N.J.: Prentice-Hall, 1976), p. 179.

accountants, college professors, engineers, schoolteachers, and nurses. They were underrepresented among clergymen and lawyers (only 54 percent of what might be expected). Today, almost 30,000 Japanese Americans work for the federal or Hawaiian government, 24,000 in Honolulu alone.

On the mainland, especially in California, there still exists a strong tradition of Japanese ownership of small businesses, so much so that there is a Los Angeles Japanese Chamber of Commerce as well as one in San Francisco. In 1958 the Los Angeles Chamber reported 6,800 businesses in 78 fields of endeavor. It was estimated that one of every seven Japanese Americans in the Los Angeles basin owned his or her own business.

Increasingly, Japanese Americans are moving into professional fields. In 1980, almost 50,000 Japanese Americans worked in executive, administrative, or managerial occupations. In addition, 20,000 were teachers, 9,000 engineers, 6,000 natural scientists, 10,000 financial consultants,

6,000 sales supervisors, and 14,000 were machinists and skilled production workers. Other common occupations included salesmen, farmers, food service, janitorial, assembly line workers, and laborers. Although they were widely represented in these occupations, most Japanese-American women held jobs as secretaries, office managers, teachers, nurses, food service workers, and assembly line workers.

LOS ANGELES BUSINESSES OWNED BY
JAPANESE AMERICANS, 1958

Type of business	Number
Private contract gardening	5,070
Apartments/Hotels	250
Grocery stores/Markets	129
Laundries/Dry cleaners	65
Gas stations	60
Insurance Agents	54
Dentists	46
Real Estate Agents	44
Florists	34
Accountants	24
Lawyers	15
Newspaper/Magazine/Book Publishers	13
Theaters	12
Opticians	11
Travel Agents	7
Doctors	5
Banks	2
Hospitals	1
Total	6,800

Source: Harry H. L. Kitano, *Japanese Americans: The Evolution of a Subculture.* 2d ed. (Englewood Cliffs, N.J.: Prentice-Hall, 1976), p. 179.

CONTRIBUTIONS TO

SOCIETY

Four generations of Japanese Americans have made many contributions to American society. The record is especially impressive when we consider that Japanese Americans have been in the United States and Canada for little more than a century. It is common to think of the Japanese today primarily in the areas of business, science, and technology, but Japan has an honored tradition of excellence in the arts, including music, literature, design, and entertainment. In these areas Japanese Americans have made many contributions. This chapter will examine some of their contributions but can not enumerate all of them.

ARCHITECTURE AND GARDENING

A long tradition of excellence in architecture has been transferred to America. In Hawaii, there are many homes built on the open style of the traditional Japanese homes, blending gardens and interior into one visual sequence. Tatami (rice straw) mats are often found in these homes, and many Japanese Americans still follow the tradition of removing their street shoes at the door and walking in the house in special sandals called *zori*. Buddhist temples and Shinto shrines have been built in Hawaii based on the traditional Japanese designs. In recent years, modern architecture has become popular with Japanese Americans.

65

The simple and elegant lines of the Friendship Knot sculpture in Little Tokyo, Los Angeles, add meaning and artistry to the landscape.

A field closely related to architecture in Japanese tradition is gardening. The great majority of contract gardeners in Southern California have been Japanese Americans and many still work with a multitude of styles. The traditional Japanese garden has been imported and is found both in large public places and many smaller home gardens, not just those belonging to Japanese Americans.

ART AND DESIGN

The Japanese Americans have excelled in many areas of art also. As in Japan, ceramic designs are favored by many Japanese-American artists, whether in the form of pottery, dinnerware, or tiles. In the area of graphic design, one of the leading American designers is Toshihiro Katayama, who has had many exhibitions around the world. A professor at Harvard University, Katayama has become one of the premier educators in the design field as well. Sculpture is another artistic field in which Japanese Americans have excelled. Sculptor Isamu Noguchi was born in Los Angeles in 1904. He studied sculpture in Japan and France, designed many stage and theater sets, and is perhaps most famous for the twenty-eight-foot-high granite cube standing on one point in front of the Marine Grace Trust Company in New York City. Another sculptor of importance is George Tsutakawa of Seattle, known for his fountains in numerous parks and buildings.

LITERATURE

Japanese literature and drama, including no and kabuki plays, are quite popular in Hawaii and other areas of the United States. Another Japanese literary influence has been in the field of poetry. There are numerous poetry groups among Japanese Americans in both the United States and Canada whose members meet to read their poems and who publish their poetry either in magazines in Japan or in *Nichi Bei Tanka* in the United States. Most of the poets write either haiku or tanka. Haiku is the shortest poetic form in the world. It has three thoughts in three lines, the first of five syllables, the second of seven, the third of five, and traditionally must mention a season of the year. Traditionally tanka has five thoughts with the first and third line having five syllables and the second, fourth, and fifth having seven syllables. Modern tanka allows some lines slightly shorter or longer and has become the most popular form in both Japan and the United States. Since no rhyming is necessary, with the syllables and thought patterns being most important, many American students in the fourth through the twelfth grades learn how to write haiku and tanka in their English classes.

Although many have been influenced by their Japanese heritage, Japanese-American writers have established their own literary voice. One author who has won acclaim for her books for children is Yoshiko Uchida. Known for her picture books about Japan as well as her novels for older children depicting Japanese-American family life during the Great Depression and World War II, Uchida has created a body of fiction that celebrates Japanese traditions while it also reflects her American heritage. A younger author who has received critical attention is David Mura. A Sansei who was born and reared in a Jewish suburb of Chicago, Mura has written poetry that focuses on such themes as wartime internment and the experiences of the Hiroshima bomb victims. In 1991, Mura published *Turning Japanese: Memoirs of a Sansei*, detailing his year-long stay in Japan on an artistic fellowship. Traveling with his Caucasian wife, Susie, Mura confronts his dual identity as a Japanese American, and his memoir records his observations about the mixing of Western and Eastern culture.

MUSIC

Music is also extremely important in Japanese society.

There are more symphony orchestras in Japan itself than in any other country. Certainly the most famous Japanese-American classical musician is Seiji Ozawa, who succeeded the famed Leonard Bernstein as the head of the Boston Symphony Orchestra following his work as a conductor with the Toronto and San Francisco Symphonies. Also famous is Toshiko Akiyoshi, who is one of the best known female jazz pianists, band leaders, and composers. The jazz fusion band Hiroshima achieved fame in the 1980's; its Japanese-American performers have appeared on several concert tours. Many Japanese Americans have learned to play the koto, sakahachi, and other traditional Japanese instruments and some of their music is now beginning to be introduced to other Americans.

ENTERTAINMENT

One of the areas in which the Japanese Americans have had most success has been movies and television, partially because so many live in Southern California. They have served as cameramen, stuntmen, directors, editors, and actors as well as many other positions. Sessue Hayakawa, who immigrated to the United States from the Chiba province of Japan shortly before World War I, appeared in the 1914 silent film, *The Typhoon*, as well as in numerous modern talking films; he is best remembered for his portrayal of the commandant of the prisoner-of-war camp in *The Bridge on the River Kwai* (1957), for which he received an Oscar nomination. The same year Miyoshi Umeki, a Japanese American, won the best supporting actress Academy Award for her work in *Sayonara*. She later appeared in *The Flower Drum Song* (1961) and as Mrs. Livingston on the television series *The Courtship of Eddie's Father*. Jack Soo (born Goro Suzuki) emerged from the relocation camps to appear in *Flower Drum Song* (1961), *Thoroughly Modern Millie* (1967), *The Green Berets* (1968), and as Nick Yemana on television's *Barney Miller*. Noriyuki

69

Typical Japanese food for the tea ceremony.

"Pat" Morita earned fame as Arnold on the television series *Happy Days* and won an Oscar nomination as best supporting actor for his work in *The Karate Kid*.

SPORTS

Certainly one of the greatest contributions to the entertainment field outside of acting by the Japanese Americans has been in the area of sports. Many of the leading instructors and practitioners of karate, judo, kendo, and other martial arts are Japanese Americans. These are traditional Japanese disciplines which often involve as much philosophy and meditation as they do active exercise. Amateur and semiprofessional sumo wrestling have also become popular in Hawaii. One of the leading figure skaters in the United States in recent years is Kristi Yamaguchi, who, in 1989, became the first skater in thirty-five years to qualify for the world championships in two events. She won the pairs championship and finished second in the women's competition.

FOOD

Japanese restaurants, found commonly in California and Hawaii, have spread throughout the United States. In the 1980's, sushi restaurants became especially popular. Most Japanese restaurants tend to specialize in one form of food such as ramen (noodles), sashimi, tempura, sukiyaki, or Kobe beef (specially fattened beef steak). Many restaurants feature Japanese chefs who cook right at the customer's table, providing elegant entertainment as well as delicious meals.

EDUCATION

Education is a highly valued goal. Children are encouraged to excel in their studies and to succeed to the best of their ability. Failure in school embarrasses the family in general. Often children attend tutoring sessions or Japanese language schools after the regular school day ends. The most prominent extra schools are the Japanese supplementary schools, usually held on Saturday, which assist the children of the kai-sha to keep up with their grade levels in Japan in language, history, culture, and mathematics.

POLITICS AND CIVIL RIGHTS

The Japanese American Citizens League (JACL), founded in 1930 in Seattle, has become one of the most successful civil rights agencies in the United States. The agency's first major challenge was the war relocation crisis; it was able to sue to obtain the right for naturalization for Issei after World War II. The JACL has been a vital force in anti-discrimination activities on the West Coast and in obtaining monetary compensation for survivors of the internment camps.

Japanese Americans in Hawaii have the kind of political influence that no other American ethnic group—with the possible exception of the Hispanic Americans in New Mexico—have achieved. They have become the dominant political group, holding most of the elected offices as governor, U.S. senators and congressmen, and state legislators, as well as other political appointments. One of these politicians is Dan Akaka, who was born in Honolulu on September 11, 1924. He was educated at the University of Hawaii, taught school, was a principal, then became director of schools in Honolulu. In 1976, he was elected to the United State House of Representatives and has served since then as a ranking member of the House Appropriations Committee. Patricia Fukuda Saiki, a Hawaiian educator of Japanese descent, entered politics as the Republican nominee for Lieutenant Governor of Hawaii in 1972 and was elected to the U.S. House of Representatives in 1986. Saiki was an official delegate to the funeral of Emperor Hirohito of Japan.

Several Japanese Americans have been elected to political office in California. Norman Yoshio Mineta was elected as mayor of San Jose, California, from 1971 to 1975, and has served in the U.S. House of Representatives from California's thirteenth district since 1975. Robert Takeo Matsui, a native of Sacramento, California, practiced law before entering the political arena. He became a member of the Sacramento City Council in 1967, vice mayor in 1977, and then ran as the Democratic candidate for the U.S. House of Representatives from the third district of California and was elected in 1979. He has served on the House Ways and Means committee.

BUSINESS

Japanese Americans entered the field of small business soon after their arrival in America. They are still prominent in the gardening, hotel, and restaurant fields. Many are leaders in other fields. Stanley Ikuo Hara is a Nisei who was born in Honolulu in 1923. A businessman who owned the Hilo Factors and the Kilauea Packing Center, Hara served from 1954 to 1978 in the state House of Representatives and Senate. Always interested in preserving the heritage of his native state, he was awarded the Grizzly Bear Award as Legislative Conservationist of the Year in 1966 by the National Wildlife Federation and the Sears-Roebuck Foundation.

FAMOUS JAPANESE

AMERICANS

There have been many notable Japanese Americans who have made contributions to American and Canadian life. The following biographical sketches represent the achievements of only a small portion of them. These individuals have been organized under their areas of achievement.

POLITICS

George Ryoichi Ariyoshi was born in Honolulu in March, 1926. He served with the famed Nisei 100th Battalion in World War II, then was educated at the University of Hawaii and received his law degree at the University of Michigan. He was elected as the territorial representative from Hawaii from 1954-1958 and then served with prominence in the Hawaiian senate. On 1974, he was the first Japanese American elected as governor of the state and served until 1986, also serving as chairman of the Western Governor's Conference.

Daniel Ken Inouye was born in Honolulu, Hawaii, on September 7, 1924. A premed student when he entered the 442nd Regimental Combat Team as a private in 1943, he lost an arm in combat in Italy and was a highly decorated captain upon his discharge in 1947. He finished his bachelors degree at the University of Hawaii and then received his law degree at George Washington University. In 1954, Inouye ran successfully for the Hawaiian House of Representatives

Mike M. Masaoka, 1958

as a Democrat. In 1959, he became one of Hawaii's original representatives in the U.S. Congress and in 1962 he was elected to the Senate, where he has served continuously since. In 1968, he gave the keynote speech at the Democratic National Convention. Inouye was one of the seven members who served on the Senate Watergate Committee, which held public hearings to investigate the Watergate affair beginning on May 17, 1973. His longest service has been on the Appropriations Committee and the Select Subcommittee on Intelligence.

A Nisei born in California in 1900, Mike Masaoka became the national secretary of the Japanese American Citizens League (JACL) in 1941. He led the fight against war relocation as the principal spokesmen of the Japanese Americans. After fighting with the famed 442nd Regimental Combat Team, he returned to become the national legislative director of the JACL Anti-Discrimination Committee in Washington. His lobbying greatly improved the lives of the Japanese Americans after the war.

Spark Masayuki Matsunaga was born in 1916 in Kauai, Hawaii. He received his bachelor of education degree from the University of Hawaii in 1941 and served with the 442nd Regimental Combat Team. His law degree came from Harvard in 1951. He served in several governmental posts under the Truman Administration and in 1954 promoted Japanese-American candidates into prominent political offices in Hawaii. From 1962 to 1976, Matsunaga was a U.S. Representative and from 1976 to 1988 he served Hawaii in the U.S. Senate.

Patsy Takemoto Mink was born in Maui, Hawaii, in 1947. She was educated at the University of Hawaii and the Chicago Law School, becoming Hawaii's first female Nisei lawyer in 1951. She was elected to the U.S. House of Representatives in 1964 and served until being named Assistant Secretary of State for Oceans and International Environment and Scientific

Affairs under the Carter Administration. Returning to Hawaii, Mink remained active in the human rights cause; she has received awards from the NAACP, Freedom Fund, and the YMCA. In 1990, she was re-elected to the U.S. House of Representatives.

EDUCATION

Samuel Ichiye Hayakawa was born in Vancouver, British Columbia, in 1906. He received his undergraduate degree from University of Manitoba, his master's degree from McGill University, and his doctorate from the University of Wisconsin in 1935. Specializing in the field of semantics, in which he was one of the world's leading experts, Dr. Hayakawa taught English at the University of Wisconsin, the Illinois Institute of Technology, and the University of Chicago before coming to San Francisco State College (now California State University, San Francisco) in 1955. He authored several important books, most notably *Language in Thought and Action*. This influential work, which went through four editions between 1949 and 1977 and was translated into ten languages, was widely used as a college text. Torn apart by faculty discontent and demands from various ethnic minorities, San Francisco State appointed Hayakawa as its president in 1968. His policy of strict discipline for both faculty and students and his crusade for academic excellence were controversial but highly successful, creating an excellent reputation for the university. In 1976, he was elected to one term as U.S. senator from California.

Harry H. L. Kitano was born on February 11, 1926, in San Francisco. He received his bachelor's degree, master's degree in social work, and doctoral degree from the University of California, Berkeley. He has taught and written extensively in the areas of sociology and social work as well as serving as the academic affirmative action officer at the UCLA. Kitano is

Seiji Ozawa, Music Director, Boston Symphony Orchestra

a prominent author on the Japanese-American experience; among his works are *Japanese Americans: The Evolution of a Subculture* (1969, 1976) and *The Japanese Americans* (1988), as well as coauthored works such as *American Racism* and *From Relocation to Redress*.

ART AND ARCHITECTURE

Born in Osaka, Japan, in 1928, Toshihiro Katayama came to the United States in 1966 to teach at the Carpenter Center for the Visual Arts of Harvard University. He has become one of the leading graphic designers in the world presenting numerous exhibitions and designing many famed magazine covers, posters, and trademarks.

Born in Seattle in 1912, Minoru Norman Yamasaki studied architecture at the University of Washington. His most outstanding buildings include the Woodrow Wilson School of Public and International Affairs of Princeton University, the Federal Science Pavilion at Seattle's Century 21 Exposition, the Dhahran Airport in Saudi Arabia, and the world's second tallest buildings, the twin towers of the World Trade Center in New York. In 1962 the Japanese American Citizens League named Yamasaki as their Nisei of the biennium for "artfully blending" Japanese art with Western architecture. Yamasaki died in 1986.

MUSIC AND ENTERTAINMENT

One of the best known women jazz musicians, Toshiko Akiyoshi was born in Manchuria in 1929 and came to the United States for her education at the Berklee College of Music in Boston. She has toured the United States, Europe, and Japan with the Toshiko Akiyoshi/Lew Tabackin Big Band since 1972. Her albums include *Long Yellow Road*, which won the Best Jazz Album of the Year in 1976. The Downbeat Poll named her the Best Arranger in 1978, 1979, and 1989, and her band as the best in 1978 and 1979.

Noriyuki "Pat" Morita was born in 1933 in Isleton, California. After performing as a character actor for several years in Hollywood, Morita earned fame in the role of Arnold on the hit television series *Happy Days*. Morita's work on television led to his casting as Mr. Miyagi, the Japanese handyman and karate master in the film *The Karate Kid* (1984). His performance earned him an Academy Award nomination as best supporting actor. Since then, Morita has starred in the two *Karate Kid* sequels and in the television series *Ohara* (1987-1988) as a Japanese-American police detective who relies on martial arts for protection.

Seiji Ozawa was born in 1935 in Hoten, Japan. Planning to be a concert pianist, he switched to conducting after he broke two of his fingers while playing soccer. Ozawa first came to the United States as an assistant conductor of the New York Philharmonic Orchestra. He then went to Tokyo's Niesei Theater and the Toronto Symphony Orchestra. From 1968 to 1973, he conducted the San Francisco Symphony. Since 1973, he has been the director of the Boston Symphony Orchestra, succeeding Leonard Bernstein.

Born in Los Angeles, George Takei was graduated from UCLA and studied drama at the Desilu studios in Hollywood. In the early 1960's he had a variety of supporting roles in television shows, including *Playhouse 90* and *The Perry Mason Show*. Takei is best known for his role as Mr. Sulu, an Asian member of the multi-ethnic crew of the U.S.S. *Enterprise*, in the original *Star Trek* television series from 1966-1969. Takei's film roles in *Ice Palace* (1960), *Walk, Don't Run* (1966), and *The Green Berets* (1968) gave him the opportunity to work with such Hollywood legends as Richard Burton, Cary Grant, and John Wayne. During the past decade, Takei has reprised his role as Sulu, appearing in *Star Trek: The Motion Picture* (1979), *Star Trek II: The Wrath of Khan*

George Takei

(1982), *Star Trek III: The Search for Spock* (1984), *Star Trek IV: The Voyage Home* (1986), *Star Trek V: The Final Frontier* (1989).

THE SCIENCES

Born to a samurai family in Japan in 1854, Jokichi Takemine chose to study chemistry rather than war. He came to the United States in 1884 and was responsible for isolating adrenalin, the first human hormone to be discovered. Takemine helped found the Japanese Association of New York and befriended many new immigrants from Japan, especially those in the arts, music, and chemistry.

Hideyo Noguchi was born in Inawashiro, Japan, in 1876. He came to America in 1899 to work in Philadelphia at the University of Pennsylvania's pathology lab. Noguchi was known for his research in yellow fever and syphilis and for studies of snake venom. He died while studying yellow fever in Africa. His birthplace in Japan has erected a shrine to his memory.

Born in Kealakekua, Kona, Hawaii, in 1946, Ellison Onizuka grew up watching the stars in Honolulu's Bishop Museum telescope. He studied aerospace engineering at the University of Colorado and worked as a Air Force test pilot and engineer, reaching the rank of lieutenant colonel. He joined the National Aeronautics and Space Administration (NASA) in 1978 and flew as a mission specialist on the *Discovery* space shuttle flight of January, 1985, which launched a secret intelligence satellite. On January 28, 1986, Onizuka was one of the seven crew members who were killed in the launch explosion of the space shuttle *Challenger*.

JOURNALISM AND LITERATURE

Born in 1883 in Okinawa and educated in Japan, Tetsuo Toyama came to the canefields of Hawaii in 1906. After

National Aeronautics and Space Administration

Ellison S. Onizuka

several years, Toyama began to publish the *Jitsugyono Hawaii Journal*, a magazine which pushed for better conditions for Japanese workers in Hawaii. He was among the first Issei to become naturalized citizens in 1953. In the following year he began a bilingual newspaper, *The Citizen*, which urged elderly Japanese to seek citizenship. Toyama was a strong supporter of this citizenship drive—he offered free citizenship classes in his office. He was beloved of all at the time of his death in 1971.

Born in Alameda, California, in 1921, Yoshiko Uchida was one of many Nisei who were sent to the internment camps during World War II. Uchida transformed her childhood experiences into two series of books, one dealing with the Depression era in California and the other with relocation to an internment camp in Utah. In addition to these books for young adults, Uchida has written several prizewinning picture books based on Japanese folk tales and other themes that incorporate the richness of her Japanese heritage.

TIME LINE

1542	First Europeans (Portuguese) arrive in Japan.
1630	Japan closed to Westerners except for Dutch trading post at Nagasaki.
1853	Commodore Matthew C. Perry of U.S. Navy begins process of opening Japan to Western influence.
1868	First Japanese arrive in Hawaii.
1869-1871	Small Japanese colony at Wakamatsu in Northern California.
1880	Census shows 148 Japanese students in the United States.
1882	Chinese Exclusion Act severely limits Chinese immigration and creates a demand in the U.S. for Japanese laborers.
1885	Japanese government begins to encourage emigration to Hawaii, the U.S., and Canada.
1886	The first Japanese arrive in Victoria, British Columbia, Canada.
1889	San Francisco *Bulletin* begins "yellow peril" campaign against Japanese immigration.
1898	The United States annexes Hawaii.
1906	The San Francisco Earthquake and its fiery aftermath devastate the Japanese area of the city.
	San Francisco School Board segregates all Oriental students to one school, resulting in protests from Japan.
1907	President Theodore Roosevelt negotiates a compromise reintegrating Japanese students in the San Francisco school system.
	Demonstrators in Vancouver, British Columbia, Canada, push for legislation to exclude Japanese immigrants. Rioters destroy Japanese-owned shops and houses.
1907-1908	Diplomatic notes bring about the Gentlemen's Agreement between the United States and Japan restricting immigration to middle- and upper-class Japanese.
	Similar agreement is negotiated between Japan and Canada.

1908-1924	The peak period of picture bride migration to the United States.
1913	California enacts Alien Land Law prohibiting "aliens ineligible for citizenship" (namely Issei) from owning land.
1924	U.S. Immigration Act effectively prohibits Japanese immigration by denying entry to those ineligible for citizenship. ,
1920-1940	Japanese farmers come to dominate much of the California production of vegetables.
1930	Japanese American Citizens League formed.
1941	Japanese attack on Pearl Harbor, Hawaii, prompts U.S. to enter World War II.
1941-1945	Nisei interpreters and cryptographers in the Intelligence section of the U.S. Army assist American efforts in the Pacific War.
1942	President Franklin Roosevelt signs Executive Order 9066 authorizing the internment of Japanese Americans on the mainland.
1942-1945	442nd Regimental Combat Team (Nisei) fights in Italy and France and becomes the most decorated regimental unit in American history.
1944	U.S. Supreme Court in *Endo* case ends legal basis of internment—the first step toward closing the camps.
1946	Proposition 15, which would have continued alien land laws in California, is defeated.
1947	Soldier's Bride Act allows U.S. soldiers to marry Japanese women and bring them to the United States.
1948	Evacuation Claims Act provides payment of settlements to Japanese Americans who suffered economic losses from internment (10 cents is paid for every $1 lost). U.S. Supreme Court allows Issei to own land.
1952	McCarran-Walter Act allowed a token immigration quota to all Asian nations (185 per year from Japan) and removed all racial barriers to naturalization as citizens.
1959	Hawaii becomes fiftieth state with Japanese Americans as the largest group. Japanese Americans enter the U.S. Congress for the first time.
1965	Immigration and Nationality Act passed by Congress marks a major shift in policy, abandoning the national-origins quota system and allowing immigration based on need for skilled workers and on principle of family reunification.

1970   Major kai-sha migration to the United States begins.
1980   President Jimmy Carter appoints seven-member commission to study legal and social implications of Japanese-American internment.
1988   Congress passes compensation bill for Japanese interned during World War II.

GLOSSARY

Edo (also spelled Yedo): The old Japanese name for Tokyo.

Haiku: A short form of Japanese poetry consisting of seventeen syllables, the first and third lines containing five syllables and the second line containing seven syllables.

Hashi: The Japanese term for chopsticks.

Hyogo: The old Japanese name for the city of Osaka

Issei: Japanese immigrants who were the first generation to live in the United States.

Judo: The Japanese art of self-defense based on self-discipline.

Meiji: The name of the Japanese imperial family which came to power in 1868.

Nichibei Shimbun: The *Japan America News*, a Japanese-language newspaper founded in San Francisco in 1899.

Nihonmachi: Literally meaning "Japantown," this term refers to the distinct communities of Japanese immigrants that sprang up in various cities on the west coast of the United States and Canada.

Nisei: Children of Japanese descent born in America to Issei parents; the second generation to live in North America.

Origami: The Japanese art of paper folding.

Ramen: Japanese noodles

Samurai: Japanese warrior-soldiers who enforced the policies of the ruling landowners during the time of the shoguns.

Sansei: Children of Japanese descent born of Nisei parents; the third generation to live in North America.

Sashimi: Raw fish; often called sushi in the United States and Canada.

Shinto: Traditional Japanese religion consisting of devotion and reverence shown to ancestors, imperial rulers, and gods of nature, particularly the sun-goddess.

Sukiyaki: Strips of beef and vegetables, including tofu, marinated in soy sauce and grilled.

Sushi: The collective name for a variety of rice dishes in which the rice is flavored with sweet vinegar and is served with vegetables, raw fish, or other seafood.

Tanka: A short form of Japanese poetry similar to haiku, but containing thirty-one syllables. The first and third lines have five syllables and the second, fourth, and fifth have seven syllables.

Tempura: A Japanese dish containing meat and vegetables dipped in batter and deep fried.

Tofu: A soft vegetable cheese formed from soybean milk and used in many Japanese dishes.

Yonsei: Children of Japanese descent born of Sansei parents; the fourth generation to live in North America.

Zen Buddhism: A Japanese sect of Buddhism that seeks spiritual enlightenment through meditation.

RESOURCES

Honolulu Japanese Chamber of Commerce
2454 S. Beretania St.
Honolulu, HI 96826
(808) 949-5581

Founded in 1900, this Chamber of Commerce supports the cultural, economic, and social activities of many Hawaiian and Japan-related community groups. Publishes an annual membership directory as well as the *Shoko Newsletter*, an annual listing of Hawaiian activities and chamber functions.

Japan Foundation
142 W. 57th St.
New York, NY 10019
(212) 949-6300

This organization, founded in 1972, sponsors international cultural and educational exchange programs. In addition to lecture series, craft demonstrations, and academic fellowships, the foundation offers financial assistance to U.S. institutions interested in creating or expanding their libraries and educational programs. Publishes a bimonthly newsletter and an annual *Bibliography for Japanese Studies*.

Japan Society
333 E. 47th St.
New York, NY 10017
(212) 832-1155

Created in 1907, this organization promotes intellectual exchange between Americans and Japanese. The society sponsors a variety of cultural programs, seminars, and courses. It offers a public affairs outreach service, maintains an extensive library, and publishes *Japan: A Reader's Guide*.

Japan-America Society of Washington
Dacor-Bacon House Mews
606 18th St. N.W.
Washington, DC 20006
(202) 289-8290

Founded in 1957, this association of American and Japanese citizens is dedicated to improving relations between their two countries. The society sponsors student exchanges, children's services, seminars, and an annual Japanese Festival. Maintains a library of works focusing on Japanese-American relations and publishes the *Bulletin* ten times per year.

Japanese American Citizens League (JACL)
1765 Sutter St.
San Francisco, CA 94115
(415) 921-5225

The league was founded in 1929 and is dedicated to protecting the civil and human rights of Japanese Americans, as well as preserving their ethnic and cultural heritage. The JACL maintains a resource library of books and audiovisual materials about Japanese Americans, sponsors athletic competitions, and grants scholarships and awards to citizens of Japanese descent.

Japanese American Curriculum Project
414 E. Third Ave.
P.O. Box 367
San Mateo, CA 94401
(415) 343-9408

This organization develops and circulates curriculum materials focused on Asian-American culture and history to schools, libraries, and Asian Americans. It also publishes an annual catalog listing books, journals, posters, games, and toys featuring Asian-American themes.

Smithsonian Institution
National Museum of American History
The Mall
Washington, D.C. 200
(202) 357-1883

A permanent exhibit entitled "A More Perfect Union: Japanese Americans and the United States Constitution" was opened in October,

1987. It deals with the experience of wartime relocation and internment, as well as the exploits of the 442nd Regimental Combat Team. The exhibit is located within the Division of Armed Forces History.

U.S.-Japan Culture Center
600 New Hampshire Ave. N.W., Suite 750
Washington, D.C. 20037
(202) 342-5800

In order to increase the awareness of U.S.-Japanese relations among students, business people, government officials, and the public, the center sponsors a variety of exchange programs and cultural activities. The center provides research services and maintains an extensive library of Japanese and American books, periodicals, and newspapers.

BIBLIOGRAPHY

Broadfoot, Barry. *Years of Sorrow, Years of Shame: The Story of Japanese Canadians in World War II*. New York: Doubleday, 1977. Oral histories by Japanese Canadians who endured internment in Canada during World War II.

Kitano, Harry H. L. *The Japanese Americans*. New York: Chelsea House, 1988. Intended for middle school and high school readers, this work provides an excellent introduction to the life of Japanese Americans and is accompanied by many fine pictures.

——————. *Japanese Americans: The Evolution of a Subculture*. 2d ed. Englewood Cliffs, N.J.: Prentice-Hall, 1976. Kitano, a professor at the University of California, Los Angeles, is the leading expert on Japanese-American life. This is a solid work but is slightly outdated.

Melendy, H. Brett. *The Oriental Americans*. New York: Twayne, 1972. A readable survey of the Chinese and Japanese experience in America to 1970. Strong on contributions of individual Asian Americans to society.

Nixon, Lucille M., and Tomoe Tana, translators. *Sounds from the Unknown: A Collection of Japanese-American Tanka*. Denver: Alan Swallow, 1963. The best collection in English of traditional Japanese poetry written by Japanese Americans in the United States and Canada.

Odo, Franklin, and Kazuko Sinoto. *A Pictorial History of the Japanese in Hawaii, 1885-1924*. Honolulu: Bishop Museum Press, 1985. Excellent black-and-white photographs illustrate the life of the earliest immigrants from Japan to the United States. This phototext emphasizes the impact of plantation life on the Japanese-American community in Hawaii.

Ogawa, Dennis M. *Kodomo No Tame Ni: For the Sake of the Children: The Japanese American Experience in Hawaii*. Honolulu: University of Hawaii Press, 1978. A report from a conference in Hawaii, this work contains solid material but is somewhat disjointed. Recommended for advanced students.

Tabrah, Ruth. *Hawaii: A Bicentennial History*. New York: W. W. Norton, 1980. A well-produced history of the fiftieth state presented in language that secondary students can understand. Excellent coverage of the early Japanese experience in Hawaii but relatively little material covers the period since 1950.

Takaki, Ronald. *Strangers from a Different Shore: A History of Asian Americans*. Boston: Little, Brown, 1989. A recent comparative study of Asian groups in America, this work has excellent coverage of the Japanese in America. Takaki, a professor at the University of California, Berkeley, is a descendent of Issei parents who were plantation workers in Hawaii.

Takashima, Shizuye. *A Child in Prison Camp*. New York: William Morrow, 1974. A talented writer and illustrator, Takashima provides an illustrated memoir based on her family's experiences in Canada during World War II. Although aimed at a juvenile audience, this poignant memoir speaks to people of all ages.

Tanaka, Michiko. *Through Harsh Winters: The Life of a Japanese Immigrant Woman*. Edited by Akemi Kikumura. Novato, Calif.: Chandler and Sharp, 1981. One of the best accounts written by a Japanese immigrant, Tanaka's diary chronicles her difficult life as a foreigner and a woman struggling to survive in America.

Vernon, Philip E. *The Abilities and Achievements of Orientals in North America*. New York: Academic Press, 1982. Written by a psychologist, this work compares the results of tests of ability and achievement administered to various Asian groups. Special emphasis is placed on the performance of Chinese Americans and Japanese Americans. This study contains some of the best material on the Japanese in Canada.

Wilson, Robert A., and Bill Hosokawa. *East to America: A History of the Japanese in the United States*. New York: William Morrow, 1980. Hosokawa, former president of the Japanese American Citizens League (JACL), instituted this survey of Japanese-American history. This study strongly emphasizes the wartime internment experience and the leadership efforts of the JACL in obtaining redress for the injustices suffered by Japanese Americans during the war and after.

MEDIA BIBLIOGRAPHY

TELEVISION

Barney Miller (1975-1982). The ensemble cast of this realistic yet comedic police series included Jack Soo (born Goro Suzuki) as Detective Sergeant Nick Yemana, an Asian-American policeman who worked in New York's Greenwich Village area.

The Courtship of Eddie's Father (1969-1972). Miyoshi Umeki played Mrs. Livingston, the Japanese-American housekeeper who cared for Eddie Corbett and his widowed father.

Gung Ho (1986-1987). The popular film was adapted for television. Gedde Watanabe reprises his role as Kaz Kazuhiro, the Japanese manager of the Assan automobile plant in America.

Happy Days (1974-1986). This series, set in Milwaukee in the 1950's, featured Pat Morita in a supporting role as Arnold, the Japanese-American owner of the drive-in restaurant where Richie Cunningham and his friends hang out.

Mr. T and Tina (1976). A short-lived situation comedy starring Pat Morita as a widowed Japanese businessman who moves from Tokyo to Chicago with his extended family (uncle, sister-in-law, and children). Complications arise from hiring an American governess/housekeeper for his children.

Ohara (1987-1988). Capitalizing on his popularity in the *Karate Kid* films, this series featured Pat Morita as a Japanese-American police detective who relies on martial arts rather than a gun for protection and is paired with a hotshot white detective.

Quincy, M.E. (1976-1983). Robert Ito played Dr. Sam Fujiyama, assistant to Quincy in the Los Angeles County coroner's office. Fujiyama and Quincy used their knowledge of forensics to solve difficult cases involving murder victims.

St. Elsewhere (1982-1986). During the first season of this critically acclaimed series, Kim Miyori portrayed Dr. Wendy Armstrong, a

Japanese-American intern on the staff of St. Eligius, a Boston-area teaching hospital.

Star Trek (1966-1969). George Takei starred as Mr. Sulu, one of the officers on the bridge and part of the multiethnic staff of the *U.S.S. Enterprise* in this well-loved series, whose popularity led to the creation of several motion pictures.

NOVELS

Clavell, James. *Shōgun: A Novel of Japan*, 1975. This two-volume historical novel, a best-seller which was subsequently made into a television miniseries, focuses on the experiences of Captain John Blackthorne, the British-born pilot of a shipwrecked Dutch trading vessel, who becomes involved in the struggle between powerful samurai competing for the position of shogun in feudal Japan.

Irwin, Hadley. *Kim/Kimi*, 1987. Half Caucasian, half Japanese, Kim leaves her home in Iowa to travel to Sacramento, California, in search of family of the dead father she never knew. After she arrives, Kim discovers her Japanese heritage, learns about her family's internment during World War II, and meets her grandmother, who still harbors bitter memories.

Kadohata, Cynthia. *The Floating World*, 1989. A short novel which chronicles the experiences of the Osaka family—twelve-year-old Olivia, her mother, her stepfather Charlie, her four brothers, and her grandmother—as they travel by automobile in the Western United States in search of employment and stability.

Miklowitz, Gloria D. *The War Between the Classes*, 1985. Emiko "Amy" Sumoto participates in a school social experiment that changes her views about her traditionalist Japanese parents, her upper-class white boyfriend, and the social prejudices that affect their relationships.

Uchida, Yoshiko. *A Jar of Dreams*, 1981, *The Best Bad Thing*, 1983, and *The Happiest Ending*, 1985. This trio of books chronicles the experiences of a Japanese-American girl named Rinko and her family as they face prejudice and learn to reach for their dreams while trying to make ends meet in Berkeley, California, during the Great Depression.

_____. *Journey to Topaz*, 1971, and *Journey Home*, 1978. Written for readers from grades five through eight, *Journey to Topaz* tells the story of hardships suffered by the Sakane family during World War II when they are sent to an internment camp in California. The sequel,

Journey Home, picks up the story with family members on parole in Salt Lake City, Utah, and concludes with their reunion with their wounded son Ken in California at the end of the war. A sensitive treatment of the racial and cultural prejudice faced by residents and citizens of Japanese descent during the war.

——————. *Samurai of Gold Hill*, 1972. Seeking a new life in California with his samurai father in the late nineteenth century, a young Japanese boy finds it difficult to adjust to the idea of being a farmer instead of a warrior.

FILMS

Come See the Paradise (1990). The internment of Japanese Americans during World War II provides the background for this love story about a union organizer (played by Dennis Quaid) and the Japanese-American woman whom he meets and marries (played by Tamlyn Tomita). Despite its flaws, this film is the first major Hollywood production to deal with the issue of the internment camps.

Gung Ho (1986). A Japanese manager and his American personnel liaison work together to help their automobile plant meet its 15,000-car production quota. Although inspired by real life events, this comedy relies on one-liners and stereotypes for its humor, but its juxtaposition of Japanese and American culture does serve to focus attention on shared characteristics as much as on cultural differences.

The Karate Kid (1984), *The Karate Kid, Part II* (1986), and *The Karate Kid III* (1989). In the original film, Noriyuki "Pat" Morita plays a Japanese-American handyman who serves as a karate mentor and surrogate father to a teenage boy who has just moved to California from the east coast. Sequels were set in Okinawa and in America and emphasized the triumph of the Oriental ideals of honor and self-reliance in the face of adversity.

Sayonara (1957). Set in Japan during the Korean War, this film deals with the racial prejudices arising from the romance between an American serviceman and a Japanese woman. Depicts the clash of rigid American military customs against the calm of Japanese tradition.

The Teahouse of the August Moon (1956). This comedy, based on a hit Broadway play, satirizes the efforts of army officers stationed in postwar Okinawa to "democratize" the Japanese inhabitants. Misperceptions on both sides are exposed and need for cross-cultural understanding is emphasized.

EDUCATIONAL FILMS

Hawaii—Her People. Filmstrip with record, cassette, and script. 55
frames. From the Hawaii Nei Series. Marsh Film Enterprises, Box
8082, Shawnee Mission, KS 66208. Includes discussion of the Japanese
experience in Hawaii.

Hawaii's People—Islands of Contrast. Filmstrip with cassette. 84 frames.
Encyclopedia Britannica Educational Audiovisuals, 425 N. Michigan
Avenue, Chicago, IL 60611. Part of the *Hawaii—50th State Series*, this
filmstrip uses the experiences of three different families in Hawaii to
show the variety of ethnic and cultural backgrounds.

The Japanese Americans. 16mm film or ½- or ¾-inch videocassette. 30
minutes. American Series number 15. Handel Film Corporation, 8730
Sunset Blvd., Hollywood, CA 90069. Portrays the history and modern
experiences of the Japanese in the United States.

Japanese Americans: An Inside Look. Filmstrip and cassette. Japanese
Curriculum Project, Inc., P.O. Box 367, San Mateo, CA 94401. This
filmstrip, distributed by an organization devoted to providing
educational materials about Japanese Americans, give an overview of
the history of Japanese Americans.

Japanese American Relocation. Kit containing two 35mm film strips, one
33⅓ phonodisk, 28 spirit masters, and other materials. Olcott Forward,
1970. Depicts the experiences of Japanese and Japanese-American
internees during World War II.

Japanese-American Relocation, 1942. Filmstrip with cassette. Educational
Audiovisuals, 29 Marble Ave., Pleasantville, NY 10570. Provides
students with a case study of the causes, consequences, and future
implications of the internment of 110,000 United States residents of
Japanese descent.

The Kyocera Experiment. 16mm film or ½-inch videocassette. 30 minutes.
Coronet/MTI Film and Video, 108 Wilmot Road, Deerfield, IL 60015.
"Theory Z" is put to the test in San Diego, where American
employees of the Kyocera Company adjust to their owners' thoroughly
Japanese style of management.

Prejudice in America: The Japanese Americans. Four filmstrips and four
cassettes. Japanese Curriculum Project, Inc., P.O. Box 367, San Mateo,
CA 94401. This series depicts the racial prejudices faced by Americans
of Japanese descent.

The Wartime Evacuation of the Japanese. Filmstrip. Social Science

School Series, 1970. Written by Harry Kitano, this filmstrip presents
another view of the internment experience during World War II.

We All Came to America. 16mm Film. 23 minutes. Kent State University
Video and Film Rental Center, Kent, Ohio 44242. Employs interviews,
photographs, prints, and motion pictures to document the story of
millions of people who left their homes to travel to the unknown
country of America. Japanese immigrants are covered as part of the
larger story of immigration to America.

There are many fine audiovisuals on Japan's history, culture, business
practices and art. One which might be of particular interest to the
students since it involves U.S.-Japanese interaction is *The Colonel Comes
to Japan*, a 30-minute presentation available on 16mm film or ½-inch
videocassette which deals with the unusual marketing challenges and
results of Kentucky Fried Chicken's entry into the Japanese fast food
market. This educational film is distributed by Coronet/MTI Film and
Video, 108 Wilmot Road, Deerfield, IL 60015.

INDEX